British Ra

LOCC

SIXTY-THIRD EDITION
2021

The complete guide to all
Locomotives which operate on
the national railway
and Eurotunnel networks

Robert Pritchard

ISBN 978 1909 431 61 4

© 2020. Platform 5 Publishing Ltd, 52 Broadfield Road, Sheffield, S8 0XJ, England.

Printed in England by The Lavenham Press, Lavenham, Suffolk.

CONTENTS

PROVISION OF INFORMATION

This book has been compiled with care to be as accurate as possible, but some information is not easily available and the publisher cannot be held responsible for any errors or omissions. We would like to thank the companies and individuals who have been helpful in supplying information to us. The authors of this series of books are always pleased to receive notification of any inaccuracies that may be found, to enhance future editions. Please send comments to:

Robert Pritchard, Platform 5 Publishing Ltd, 52 Broadfield Road, Sheffield, S8 0XJ, England.

e-mail: robert.pritchard@platform5.com **Tel:** 0114 255 2625.

This book is updated to information received by 12 October 2020.

UPDATES

This book is updated to the Stock Changes given in **Today's Railways UK 225** (November 2020). The Platform 5 railway magazine "**Today's Railways UK**" publishes Stock Changes every month to update this book. The magazine also contains news and rolling stock information on the railways of Great Britain and Ireland and is published on the second Monday of every month. For further details of **Today's Railways UK**, please contact Platform 5 Publishing Ltd or visit our website **www.platform5.com**.

Front cover photograph: Great Western Railway green-liveried 57603 "Tintagel Castle" passes Hungerford Common with a rake of empty GWR Sleeper stock running from Penzance to Reading on 14/04/20. **Tony Bartlett**

BRITAIN'S RAILWAY SYSTEM

The structure of Britain's railway system changed significantly during 2020, following the ongoing Covid-19 pandemic which saw passenger numbers drop by around 60–70% across the country. This drop in passenger numbers meant that franchises were no longer profitable and the Government was forced to step in and provide financial support to operators. Initially in March 2020 the Transport Secretary suspended rail franchising and operators transitioned to "Emergency Measures Agreements". These EMAs suspended the normal financial agreements, instead transferring all revenue and cost risk to the Government. The existing operators in England all accepted these new arrangements and continued to operate trains (initially with reduced service frequencies) for a small management fee. Similar arrangements were put in place by the Scottish and Welsh Governments for ScotRail, Caledonian Sleeper and Transport for Wales.

The EMAs initially lasted for six months until September 2020, from which time longer "Emergency Recovery Management Agreements" (ERMAs) were put in place. These were similar management contracts which continued to see operators run services for a management fee. In the longer term the franchise model is expected to be changed to one of concessions, although this is expected to take several years to fully implement.

In London and on Merseyside concessions were already in place. Concessions see the operator paid a fee to run the service, usually within tightly specified guidelines. Operators running a concession would not normally take commercial risks, although there are usually penalties and rewards in the contract.

Britain's national railway infrastructure is owned by a "not for dividend" company, Network Rail. In 2014 Network Rail was reclassified as a public sector company, being described by the Government as a "public sector arm's-length body of the Department for Transport".

Most stations and maintenance depots are leased to and operated by Train Operating Companies (TOCs), but some larger stations are controlled by Network Rail. The only exception is the infrastructure on the Isle of Wight: The Island Line franchise uniquely included maintenance of the infrastructure as well as the operation of passenger services. As Island Line is now part of South Western Railway, both the infrastructure and trains are operated by SWR.

Trains are operated by TOCs over Network Rail tracks (the National Network), regulated by access agreements between the parties involved. In general, TOCs are responsible for the provision and maintenance of the trains and staff necessary for the direct operation of services, whilst Network Rail is responsible for the provision and maintenance of the infrastructure and also for staff to regulate the operation of services.

The Department for Transport (DfT) is the franchising authority for the national network, with Transport Scotland overseeing the award of the ScotRail and Caledonian Sleeper franchises and the Welsh Government overseeing the Wales & Borders franchise.

Now superceded by the ERMAs, each franchise was set up with the right to run specified services within a specified area for a period of time, in return for the right to charge fares and, where appropriate, to receive financial support from the Government. Subsidy was payable in respect of socially necessary services. Service standards are monitored by the DfT throughout the duration of the franchise. Franchisees earned revenue primarily from fares and from subsidy. They generally leased stations from Network Rail and earned rental income by sub-letting parts of them, for example to retailers.

TOC's and open access operator's main costs are the track access charges they pay to Network Rail, the costs of leasing stations and rolling stock and of employing staff. Franchisees may do light maintenance work on rolling stock or contract it out to other companies. Heavy maintenance is normally carried out by the Rolling Stock Leasing Companies, according to contracts.

Note that a railway "reporting period" is four weeks.

DOMESTIC PASSENGER TRAIN OPERATORS

The majority of passenger trains are operated by Train Operating Companies, now supported by the Government through the Emergency Recovery Management Agreements, which have replaced franchises. These generally run for between six and 18 months. Caledonian Sleeper, ScotRail and Transport for Wales are still operating under Emergency Measures Agreements (EMAs) pending longer support deals being signed. For reference the date of the expiry of the original franchise is also given here.

Name of franchise	*Operator*	*Trading Name*
Caledonian Sleeper	Serco	**Caledonian Sleeper**

EMA until 10 January 2021; original franchise was until 31 March 2030

The Sleeper franchise started in April 2015 when operation of the ScotRail and ScotRail Sleeper franchises was separated. Abellio won the ScotRail franchise and Serco the Caledonian Sleeper franchise. Caledonian Sleeper operates four trains nightly between London Euston and Scotland using locomotives hired from GBRf. New CAF Mark 5 rolling stock was introduced during 2019.

Chiltern	Arriva (Deutsche Bahn)	**Chiltern Railways**

EMRA until 11 December 2021, the original franchise expiry date

Chiltern Railways operates a frequent service between London Marylebone, Oxford, Banbury and Birmingham Snow Hill, with some peak trains extending to Kidderminster. There are also regular services from Marylebone to Stratford-upon-Avon and to Aylesbury Vale Parkway via Amersham (along the London Underground Metropolitan Line). The fleet consists of DMUs of Classes 165, 168 and 172 plus a number of locomotive-hauled rakes used on some of the Birmingham and Oxford route trains, worked by Class 68s hired from DRS.

Cross Country	Arriva (Deutsche Bahn)	**CrossCountry**

EMRA until 15 October 2023; original franchise expired on 17 October 2020

CrossCountry operates a network of long distance services between Scotland, the North-East of England and Manchester to the South-West of England, Reading, Southampton, Bournemouth and Guildford, centred on Birmingham New Street. These trains are mainly formed of diesel Class 220/221 Voyagers, supplemented by a small number of HSTs on the NE–SW route. Inter-urban services also link Nottingham, Leicester and Stansted Airport with Birmingham and Cardiff. These trains use Class 170 DMUs.

Crossrail

| | MTR | **TfL Rail** |

Concession until 27 May 2023 (with an option to extend the concession by 2 years to May 2025)

This concession started in May 2015. Initially Crossrail took over the Liverpool Street–Shenfield stopping service from Greater Anglia, using a fleet of Class 315 EMUs, with the service branded "TfL Rail". New Class 345 EMUs are being introduced on this route and are also now used between Paddington and Hayes & Harlington and Paddington and Reading (some initially in 7-car formation). TfL Rail currently also operates the former Heathrow Connect stopping service that now also uses Class 345s. The opening of Crossrail through central London has been delayed and operation through new tunnels beneath central London, from Shenfield and Abbey Wood in the east to Reading and Heathrow Airport in the west is now expected in late 2021 or early 2022. It will then be branded the "Elizabeth Line".

East Coast

| | DfT | **London North Eastern Railway** |

Operated by DfT's "Operator of Last Resort" until June 2023

LNER operates frequent long distance trains on the East Coast Main Line between London King's Cross, Leeds, Lincoln, Harrogate, York, Newcastle-upon-Tyne and Edinburgh, with less frequent services to Bradford, Skipton, Hull, Glasgow, Stirling, Aberdeen and Inverness. A new fleet of 65 Hitachi Class 800 and 801 "Azuma" trains have all now been introduced (these are a mix of bi-mode and electric, 5- and 9-car units) and operate the majority of services. A small number of Class 91+Mark 4 sets have been retained until at least 2023 and are mainly used on Leeds and York services.

East Midlands

| | Abellio | **East Midlands Railway** |

ERMA until 31 March 2022; original franchise was until 21 August 2027

EMR operates a mix of long distance high speed services on the Midland Main Line (MML), from London St Pancras to Sheffield (to Leeds at peak times and with some extensions to York), Nottingham (plus peak-hour trains to Lincoln) and Corby, and local and regional services ranging from the long distance Norwich–Liverpool route to Nottingham–Skegness, Nottingham–Mansfield–Worksop, Newark–Matlock and Derby–Crewe. It also operates local services across Lincolnshire. Trains on the MML are worked by a fleet of Class 222 DMUs and HSTs, whilst the local and regional fleet consists of DMU Classes 153, 156 and 158. In 2021 Class 360 EMUs will join the fleet to operate services on the newly electrified St Pancras–Corby route from May 2021. Four former Hull Trains Class 180s are also being leased to operate some services on the MML.

East Anglia

| | Abellio (Netherlands Railways) (60%)/Mitsui Group (40%) | **Greater Anglia** |

ERMA until 18 September 2021; original franchise was until 11 October 2025

Greater Anglia operates main line trains between London Liverpool Street, Ipswich and Norwich and local trains across Norfolk, Suffolk and parts of Cambridgeshire. It also runs local and commuter services into Liverpool Street from the Great Eastern (including Southend, Braintree and Clacton) and West Anglia (including Ely/Cambridge and Stansted Airport) routes. In 2019–20 a new fleet of Stadler EMUs and bi-mode units (Classes 745 and 755) was introduced on the GEML and in East Anglia, replacing older DMUs and loco-hauled trains. Classes 317, 321, 322, 360 and 379 EMUs are still operated out of Liverpool Street and will be replaced by a large fleet of new Class 720 Aventras in 2020–22.

Essex Thameside   Trenitalia   **c2c**
ERMA until 31 March 2021; original franchise was until 10 November 2029

c2c operates an intensive, principally commuter, service from London Fenchurch Street to Southend and Shoeburyness via both Upminster and Tilbury. The fleet consists of 74 Class 357 EMUs, plus six Class 387s.

Great Western   First Group   **Great Western Railway**
ERMA until 26 June 2021; original franchise was until 31 March 2023

Great Western Railway operates long distance trains from London Paddington to South Wales, the West Country and Worcester and Hereford. In addition there are frequent trains along the Thames Valley corridor to Newbury/Bedwyn and Oxford, plus local and regional trains throughout the South-West including the Cornish, Devon and Thames Valley branches, the Reading–Gatwick North Downs Line and Cardiff–Portsmouth Harbour and Bristol–Weymouth regional routes. Long distance services are now in the hands of a new fleet of Class 800/802 bi-mode InterCity Express Trains. DMUs of Classes 165 and 166 are used on the Thames Valley branches and North Downs routes as well as on local services around Bristol and across to Cardiff. Class 387 EMUs are used between Paddington, Reading, Didcot Parkway and Newbury. Classes 143, 150 and 158 and a fleet of short 4-car HSTs are used on local and regional trains in the South-West. A small fleet of Class 57s is maintained to work the overnight "Cornish Riviera" Sleeper service between London Paddington and Penzance formed of Mark 3 coaches.

London Rail   Arriva (Deutsche Bahn)   **London Overground**
Concession until 25 May 2024 (with an option to extend the concession by 2 years to May 2026)

London Overground operates services on the Richmond–Stratford North London Line and the Willesden Junction–Clapham Junction West London Line, plus the East London Line from Highbury & Islington to New Cross and New Cross Gate, with extensions to Clapham Junction (via Denmark Hill), Crystal Palace and West Croydon. It also runs services from London Euston to Watford Junction. All these use Class 378 EMUs, with new Class 710s also recently introduced onto the Watford Junction route. Class 710s also operate services on the Gospel Oak–Barking line. London Overground also operates some suburban services from London Liverpool Street – to Chingford, Enfield Town and Cheshunt. From autumn 2020 these services all use Class 710s, with one unit also used on the Romford–Upminster shuttle.

Merseyrail Electrics   Serco (50%)/Abellio (Netherlands Railways) (50%)   **Merseyrail**
Concession until 22 July 2028. Under the control of Merseytravel PTE instead of the DfT
Due to be reviewed every five years to fit in with the Merseyside Local Transport Plan

Merseyrail operates services between Liverpool and Southport, Ormskirk, Kirkby, Hunts Cross, New Brighton, West Kirby, Chester and Ellesmere Port, using Class 507 and 508 EMUs. A new fleet of Class 777 EMUs will be introduced from 2021.

Northern   DfT   **Northern**
Operated by DfT's "Operator of Last Resort" until further notice

Northern operates a range of inter-urban, commuter and rural services throughout the North of England, including those around the cities of Leeds, Manchester, Sheffield, Liverpool and Newcastle. The network extends from Chathill in the north to Nottingham in the south, and Cleethorpes in the east to St Bees in the west. Long distance services include Leeds–Carlisle, Morpeth–Carlisle and York–Blackpool North. The operator uses a large fleet of DMUs of Classes 142, 150, 153, 155, 156, 158, 170 and 195 plus EMU Classes 319, 323, 331 and 333. The new fleets of DMUs (Class 195) and EMUs (Class 331) have now been introduced on a number of routes, and will be followed by Class 769 bi-mode diesel electric units (converted from Class 319s). A small number of Class 142 Pacers remain in service around the North-West.

ScotRail
Abellio (Netherlands Railways) **ScotRail**
EMA until 10 January 2021; original franchise was until 31 March 2022

ScotRail provides almost all passenger services in Scotland and also trains from Glasgow to Carlisle via Dumfries, some of which extend to Newcastle-upon-Tyne (jointly operated with Northern). The company operates a large fleet of DMUs of Classes 156, 158 and 170 and EMU Classes 318, 320, 334, 380 and 385. A fleet of 26 refurbished HSTs are being introduced onto InterCity services between Edinburgh/Glasgow and Aberdeen and Inverness and also between Inverness and Aberdeen. In 2021 five Class 153s are also due to be introduced on the West Highland Line to provide more capacity and space for bikes and other luggage.

South Eastern
Govia (Go-Ahead/Keolis) **Southeastern**
EMRA until 16 October 2021; original franchise expired on 1 April 2020

Southeastern operates all services in the south-east London suburbs, the whole of Kent and part of Sussex, which are primarily commuter services to London. It also operates domestic High Speed trains on HS1 from London St Pancras to Ashford, Ramsgate, Dover and Faversham with additional peak services on other routes. EMUs of Classes 375, 376, 377, 465 and 466 are used, along with Class 395s on the High Speed trains. From 2021 the 30 Class 707 EMUs, sub-leased from South Western Railway, will also be introduced.

South Western
First Group (70%)/MTR (30%) **South Western Railway**
ERMA until 31 March 2021; original franchise ran until 17 August 2024

South Western Railway operates trains from London Waterloo to destinations across the South and South-West including Woking, Basingstoke, Southampton, Portsmouth, Salisbury, Exeter, Reading and Weymouth, as well as suburban services from Waterloo. SWR also runs services between Ryde and Shanklin on the Isle of Wight, using former London Underground 1938 stock (Class 483s). The rest of the fleet consists of DMU Classes 158 and 159 and EMU Classes 442, 444, 450, 455, 456, 458 and 707. A new fleet of Bombardier Class 701s are being delivered to replace Classes 455, 456, 458 and 707 in 2021–22. A fleet of five third rail Vivarail units (converted former LU D78 stock) is also under construction to replace the 1938 Stock on the Isle of Wight in 2021.

Thameslink, Southern & Great Northern (TSGN)
Govia (Go-Ahead/Keolis) **Govia Thameslink Railway**
ERMA until 18 September 2021, the original franchise expiry date

TSGN is the largest operator in Great Britain (the former Southern franchise was combined with Thameslink/Great Northern in 2015). GTR uses four brands: "Thameslink" for trains between Cambridge North, Peterborough, Bedford and Rainham, Sevenoaks, East Grinstead, Brighton, Littlehampton and Horsham via central London and also on the Sutton/Wimbledon loop using new Class 700 EMUs. "Great Northern" comprises services from London King's Cross and Moorgate to Welwyn Garden City, Hertford North, Peterborough, Cambridge and King's Lynn using Class 365, 387 and 717 EMUs. "Southern" operates predominantly commuter services between London, Surrey and Sussex and "metro" services in South London, as well as services along the south Coast between Southampton, Brighton, Hastings and Ashford, plus the cross-London service from South Croydon to Milton Keynes. Class 171 DMUs are used on Ashford–Eastbourne and London Bridge–Uckfield services, whilst all other services are in the hands of Class 313, 377, 455 and 700 EMUs. Finally, Gatwick Express operates non-stop trains between London Victoria, Gatwick Airport and Brighton using Class 387/2 EMUs.

Trans-Pennine Express   First Group   **TransPennine Express**
ERMA until 31 March 2021; original franchise ran until 31 March 2023

TransPennine Express operates predominantly long distance inter-urban services linking major cities across the North of England, along with Edinburgh and Glasgow in Scotland. The main services are Manchester Airport/Manchester Piccadilly–Newcastle/Redcar Central/Hull plus Liverpool–Scarborough and Liverpool–Newcastle–Edinburgh along the North Trans-Pennine route via Huddersfield, Leeds and York, and Manchester Airport–Cleethorpes along the South Trans-Pennine route via Sheffield. TPE also operates Manchester Airport–Edinburgh/Glasgow and Liverpool–Glasgow. The fleet consists of Class 185 DMUs, plus three new fleets: Class 68s+Mark 5A sets being used, or to be used on Liverpool–Scarborough and Manchester Airport–Redcar Central, Class 397s used on Manchester Airport/Liverpool–Scotland and Class 802 bi-mode units used on Liverpool–Edinburgh and Manchester Airport–Newcastle.

Wales & Borders   KeolisAmey   **Transport for Wales**
EMA until 30 November 2020; original franchise ran until 15 October 2033

Transport for Wales was procured by the Welsh Government and operates a mix of long distance, regional and local services throughout Wales, including the Valley Lines network of lines around Cardiff, and also through services to the English border counties and to Manchester and Birmingham. The fleet consists of DMUs of Classes 142, 143, 150, 153, 158, 170 and 175 and three locomotive-hauled Mark 4 sets, to be introduced in late 2020/early 2021 on the Cardiff–Holyhead route. Rebuilt Class 230 D-Trains are to be introduced on the Wrexham–Bidston line from 2021 and new Stadler and CAF fleets will be introduced on other routes from 2022.

West Coast Partnership   First Group (70%)/Trenitalia (30%)   **Avanti West Coast**
ERMA until 31 March 2022; original franchise ran until 31 March 2031

Avanti West Coast operates long distance services along the West Coast Main Line from London Euston to Birmingham/Wolverhampton, Manchester, Liverpool, Blackpool North and Glasgow using Class 390 Pendolino EMUs. It also operates Class 221 Voyagers on the Euston–Chester–Holyhead route and a small number of trains from Wolverhampton to Shrewsbury and to Wrexham, whilst a mix of Class 221s and 390s are used on the Euston–Birmingham–Glasgow/Edinburgh route.

West Midlands Trains   Abellio (70%)/JR East (15%)/Mitsui (15%)   **West Midlands Railway/**
London Northwestern
ERMA until 18 September 2021; original franchise ran until 31 March 2026

West Midlands Trains operates services under two brand names. West Midlands Railway trains are local and regional services around Birmingham, including to Stratford-upon-Avon, Worcester, Hereford, Redditch, Rugeley and Shrewsbury. WMR is managed by a consortium of 16 councils and the Department for Transport. London Northwestern is the brand used for long distance and regional services from London Euston to Northampton and Birmingham/Crewe and also between Birmingham and Liverpool, Bedford–Bletchley and Watford Junction–St Albans Abbey. The fleet consists of DMU Classes 139, 153, 170 and 172 and EMU Classes 319, 323 and 350. Class 230 D-Trains were introduced onto the Bedford–Bletchley route in 2019 and new CAF DMUs and Bombardier EMUs will also be introduced on a number of routes in 2021–22.

NON-FRANCHISED SERVICES

The following operators run non-franchised, or "open access" services (* special seasonal services):

Operator	Trading Name	Route
Heathrow Airport Holdings	Heathrow Express	London Paddington–Heathrow Airport

Heathrow Express is a frequent express passenger service between London Paddington and Heathrow Airport using Class 332 EMUs (from late 2020 Class 387s), now operated by GWR as part of its franchise.

Hull Trains (part of First)	Hull Trains	London King's Cross–Hull

Before the Covid-19 pandemic Hull Trains operated seven trains a day on weekdays from Hull to London King's Cross via the East Coast Main Line. New bi-mode Class 802s were introduced in late 2019/early 2020, replacing the Class 180 DMUs. One train in each direction starts back from and extends to Beverley. During the Covid-19 lockdown HT stopped running services, but reintroduced a limited timetable from August 2020.

Grand Central (part of Arriva)	Grand Central	London King's Cross–Sunderland/ Bradford Interchange

Grand Central operates five trains a day from Sunderland and four trains a day from Bradford Interchange to London King's Cross using Class 180 DMUs. Grand Central also planned to introduce a service between King's Cross and Blackpool in 2020, but in the light of drop in passengers caused by the Covid-19 pandemic these plans were dropped – but not before four sets of Mark 4s had been refurbished and repainted into GC livery.

Locomotive Services (TOC)	Locomotive Services	

Locomotive Services runs various excursions across the network using diesel, electric and steam locomotives operating under the brands Saphos Trains (principally steam-hauled trips), Statesman Rail (diesel-locomotive hauled trips and land cruises), Rail Charter Services (regular summer diesel-hauled trips over the Settle & Carlisle Line), Midland Pullman (HST tours) and Intercity (electric locomotive-hauled tours).

North Yorkshire Moors Railway Enterprises	North Yorkshire Moors Railway	Pickering–Grosmont–Whitby/ Battersby, Sheringham–Cromer*

The North Yorkshire Moors Railway operates services on the national network between Grosmont and Whitby or Grosmont and Battersby as an extension of its Pickering–Grosmont services and also operates services between Sheringham and Cromer on behalf of the North Norfolk Railway.

South Yorkshire Supertram	Stagecoach Supertram	Meadowhall South–Rotherham Parkgate

South Yorkshire Supertram holds a passenger licence to allow the operation of the pilot tram-train service linking Sheffield city centre with Rotherham Central and Rotherham Parkgate.

Tyne & Wear PTE	Tyne & Wear Metro	Pelaw–Sunderland

Tyne & Wear Passenger Transport Executive holds a passenger license to allow the operation of its Metro service over Network Rail tracks between Pelaw and Sunderland.

Vintage Trains	Vintage Trains	Birmingham Snow Hill–Stratford-upon-Avon*

Vintage Trains operates steam-hauled services on a seasonal basis.

West Coast Railway Company	West Coast Railway Company	Fort William–Mallaig* York–Settle–Carlisle* Carnforth–York–Scarborough*

WCRC operates steam-hauled services on these routes on a seasonal basis and a range of other excursions across the network, including the Northern Belle luxury train.

INTERNATIONAL PASSENGER OPERATORS

Eurostar International operates passenger services between London St Pancras and mainland Europe. The company, established in 2010, is jointly owned by SNCF (the national operator of France): 55%, SNCB (the national operator of Belgium): 5% and Patina Rail: 40%. Patina Rail is made up of Canadian-based Caisse de dépôt et placement du Québec (CDPG) and UK-based Hermes Infrastructure (owning 30% and 10% respectively). This 40% was previously owned by the UK Government until it was sold in 2015.

In addition, a service for the conveyance of accompanied road vehicles through the Channel Tunnel is provided by the tunnel operating company, Eurotunnel. All Eurotunnel services are operated in top-and-tail mode by the powerful Class 9 Bo-Bo-Bo locomotives.

FREIGHT TRAIN OPERATORS

The following operators operate freight services or empty passenger stock workings under "Open Access" arrangements:

Colas Rail: Colas Rail operates a number of On-Track Machines and also supplies infrastructure monitoring trains for Network Rail. It also operates a number of different freight flows, including oil and timber. Colas Rail has a small but varied fleet consisting of Class 37s, 56s, 66s, 67s and 70s.

DB Cargo (UK): Still the biggest freight operator in the country, DBC (EWS until bought by Deutsche Bahn, when it was initially called DB Schenker) provides a large number of infrastructure trains to Network Rail and also operates coal, steel, intermodal and aggregate trains nationwide. The core fleet is Class 66s. Of the original 250 ordered, 79 have moved to DB's French and Polish operations, although some of the French locos do return to the UK when major maintenance is required. Around 20–22 Class 60s are also used on heavier trains, the remainder of the fleet has been stored or sold, although DB Cargo is still responsible for the maintenance of GBRf and DCR Class 60s at Toton.

DBC's fleet of Class 67s are used on passenger or standby duties for Transport for Wales and LNER and also on excursions or special trains. Class 90s see some use on West Coast Main Line freight traffic. The Class 92s are mainly used on a limited number of overnight freights on High Speed 1.

DBC also operates the Class 325 EMUs for Royal Mail and a number of excursion trains.

Devon & Cornwall Railways (part of Cappagh Construction Contractors (London)): DCRail specialises in short-term freight haulage contracts, using Class 56s or four Class 60s acquired from DB Cargo.

Direct Rail Services: DRS has built on its original nuclear flask traffic to operate a number of different services. The main flows are intermodal plus the provision of crews and locomotives to Network Rail for autumn RailHead Treatment Trains and also infrastructure trains. DRS has a varied fleet of locomotives, with Class 20s, 37s, 57s and 66s working alongside new Class 68s and diesel-electric Class 88s. Class 68s are hired to Chiltern Railways and TransPennine Express for passenger work. Its Class 68s are also used on some excursion work.

Freightliner: Freightliner (owned by Genesee & Wyoming) operates container trains from the main Ports at Southampton, Felixstowe, Tilbury and Thamesport to major cities including London, Manchester, Leeds and Birmingham. It also operates trains of coal, cement, infrastructure and aggregates. Most services are worked by Class 66s, with Class 70s mainly used on some of the heavier intermodal trains and cement trains from the Peak District. A small fleet of Class 86 and 90 electrics are used on intermodal trains on the Great Eastern and West Coast Main Lines, the Class 86s mainly being used in pairs on the WCML between Crewe and Coatbridge. Recently introduced Class 90s that were previously operated by Greater Anglia are starting to replace some Class 86s.

The six Class 59/2s were purchased from DBC and are used alongside the Mendip Rail 59/0s and 59/1s on stone traffic from the Mendip quarries and around the South-East.

GB Railfreight: GBRf (owned by Infracapital) operates a mixture of traffic types, mainly using Class 66s together with a small fleet of Class 73s on infrastructure duties and test trains in the South-East and ten Class 60s acquired from Colas Rail in 2018. The company has also now purchased a number of Class 56s and owns a single Class 59, 59003. Some of the Class 56s are being rebuilt as Class 69s with a new GM engine. A fleet of Class 92s is also used on some intermodal flows to and from Dollands Moor or through the Channel Tunnel to Calais. Traffic includes coal, intermodal, biomass, aggregates and gypsum as well as infrastructure services for Network Rail and London Underground. GBRf also supplies Class 73/9s and Class 92s to Caledonian Sleeper and owns the three former Colas Rail Class 47s.

GBRf also operates some excursion trains, including those using the preserved Class 201 "Hastings" DEMU.

Loram (UK): Loram has a freight license and operates a limited number of trains, most hauling On-Track Machines using hired-in locomotives.

Rail Operations Group: This company mainly facilitates rolling stock movements by providing drivers or using locomotives hired from other companies or by using its own fleet of Class 47s or Class 37s hired from Europhoenix or Class 57s hired from DRS.

West Coast Railway Company: WCRC has a freight licence but doesn't operate any freight as such – only empty stock movements. Its fleet of Class 47s, supplemented by a smaller number of Class 33s, 37s and 57s, is used on excursion work nationwide.

In addition, Amey, Balfour Beatty Rail, Harsco Rail, Swietelsky Babcock Rail (SB Rail) and VolkerRail operate trains formed of On-Track Machines.

INTRODUCTION

This book contains details of all locomotives which can run on Britain's national railway network, plus those of Eurotunnel.

Locomotives currently approved for use on the national railway network fall into the four broad types: passenger, freight, mixed traffic and shunting.

Passenger
The number of dedicated passenger locomotives has not changed significantly in recent years. Classes 43 (HST) and 91 and some members of Classes 57, 67, 68, 73/9 and 92 are dedicated to franchised and Open Access passenger operations. Excursion trains have a few dedicated locomotives but mainly use locomotives that are best described as mixed traffic.

Freight
By far the most numerous locomotives are those used solely for bulk commodity and intermodal freight. Since 1998 a large number of new Class 66 locomotives have replaced many former BR designs and in more recent years smaller numbers of Class 70s have also been introduced. There are however a significant number of BR era Class 20, 37, 47, 56, 60, 73/1, 86, 90 and 92 locomotives still in use; their number has increased slightly as some locomotives have been reinstated to cope with demand. In addition there is a small fleet of Class 59s acquired privately in the 1980s and 1990s and a small number of re-engined Class 57s in use.

Mixed Traffic
In addition to their use on passenger and commodity freight workings these locomotives are used for stock movements and specialist infrastructure and test trains. The majority, but not all, are fitted with Electric Train Supply. Locomotives from Classes 20, 33, 37, 47, 57, 67, 68, 73/9, 88 and 90 fall into this category. Also included under this heading are preserved locomotives permitted to operate on the national railway network. Although these have in the past solely operated excursion trains they are increasingly seeing occasional use on other types of trains. Some, such as Class 50s with GB Railfreight, are frequently used by the main freight companies.

Shunting
Very few shunting locomotives are now permitted to operate freely on the National Railway network. The small number that are have to be fitted with a plethora of safety equipment in order to have engineering acceptance. They are mainly used for local workings such as trips between yards or stock movements between depots and stations. Otherwise, shunting locomotives are not permitted to venture from depots or yards onto the National Railway network other than into defined limits within interface infrastructure. Remotely-controlled driverless shunters are not included in this book. However, all ex-BR shunting locomotives are listed under Section 1.1 "Diesel Shunting Locomotives".

Locomotives which are owned by, for example, DB Cargo or Freightliner, which have been withdrawn from service and are awaiting disposal are listed in the main part of the book. Locomotives which are awaiting disposal at scrapyards are listed in the "Locomotives Awaiting Disposal" section.

Only preserved locomotives which are currently used on the National Railway network are included. Others, which may still be Network Rail registered but not at present certified for use, are not included, but can be found in the Platform 5 book, "Preserved Locomotives of British Railways".

LAYOUT OF INFORMATION

Locomotive classes are listed in numerical order of class. Principal details and dimensions are quoted for each class in metric and/or imperial units as considered appropriate bearing in mind common UK usage.

The heading "Total" indicates how many of that particular class are listed in this book.

Where numbers actually carried are different from those officially allocated, these are noted in class headings where appropriate. Where locomotives have been recently renumbered, the most immediate previous number is shown in parentheses. Each entry is laid out as in the following example:

No.   Detail Livery Owner Pool   Allocn.   Name
60091 +*   **DB**   DB   WCBT   TO   Barry Needham

Detail Differences. Only detail differences which currently affect the areas and types of train which locomotives may work are shown. Where such differences occur within a class or part class, they are shown in the "Detail" column alongside the individual locomotive number.

Codes: Codes are used to denote the livery, owner, pool and depot of each locomotive. Details of these will be found in section 6 of this book.

The owner is the responsible custodian of the locomotive and this may not always be the legal owner. Actual ownership can be very complicated. Some vehicles are owned by finance/leasing companies. Others are owned by subsidiary companies of a holding company or by an associate company of the responsible custodian or operator.

Depot allocation codes for all locomotives are shown in this book (apart from shunting locomotives where the actual location of each is shown). It should be noted that today much locomotive maintenance is undertaken away from these depots. This may be undertaken at fuelling points, berthing sidings or similar, or by mobile maintenance teams. Therefore locomotives in particular may not return to their "home" depots as often as in the past.

(S) denotes that the locomotive is stored (the actual location is shown).

Names: Only names carried with official sanction are listed. Names are shown in UPPER/lower case characters as actually shown on the name carried on the locomotive.

GENERAL INFORMATION

CLASSIFICATION AND NUMBERING

All locomotives are classified and allocated numbers under the TOPS numbering system, introduced in 1972. This comprises a two-digit class number followed by a three-digit serial number.

For diesel locomotives, class numbers offer an indication of engine horsepower as shown in the table below.

Class No. Range	Engine hp
01–14	0–799
15–20	800–1000
21–31	1001–1499
32–39	1500–1999
40–54, 57	2000–2999
55–56, 58–70	3000+

For electric locomotives class numbers are allocated in ascending numerical order under the following scheme:

Class 71–80   Direct current and DC/diesel dual system locomotives.
Class 81 onwards   Alternating current and AC/DC dual system locomotives.

Numbers in the 89101–89999 series are allocated to locomotives which have been deregistered but subsequently re-registered for use on the national railway network and whose original number has already been reused. These numbers are normally only carried inside locomotive cabs and are not carried externally in normal circumstances.

WHEEL ARRANGEMENT

For main line locomotives the number of driven axles on a bogie or frame is denoted by a letter (A = 1, B = 2, C = 3 etc) and the number of non-powered axles is denoted by a number. The use of the letter "o" after a letter indicates each axle is individually powered, whilst the "+" symbol indicates bogies are inter-coupled.

For shunting locomotives, the Whyte notation is used. In this notation the number of leading wheels are given, followed by the number of driving wheels and then the trailing wheels.

UNITS OF MEASUREMENT

All dimensions and weights are quoted for locomotives in an "as new" condition with all necessary supplies (eg oil, water and sand) on board. Dimensions are quoted in the order length x width. Lengths quoted are over buffers or couplers as appropriate. All widths quoted are maxima. Where two different wheel diameter dimensions are shown, the first refers to powered wheels and the second refers to non-powered wheels. All weights are shown as metric tonnes (t = tonnes).

HAULAGE CAPABILITY OF DIESEL LOCOMOTIVES

The haulage capability of a diesel locomotive depends upon three basic factors:

1. Adhesive weight. The greater the weight on the driving wheels, the greater the adhesion and more tractive power can be applied before wheelslip occurs.

2. The characteristics of its transmission. To start a train the locomotive has to exert a pull at standstill. A direct drive diesel engine cannot do this, hence the need for transmission. This may be mechanical, hydraulic or electric. The present British Standard for locomotives is electric transmission. Here the diesel engine drives a generator or alternator and the current produced is fed to the traction motors. The force produced by each driven wheel depends on the current in its traction motor. In other words, the larger the current, the harder it pulls. As the locomotive speed increases, the current in the traction motor falls, hence the *Maximum Tractive Effort* is the maximum force at its wheels the locomotive can exert at a standstill. The electrical equipment cannot take such high currents for long without overheating. Hence the *Continuous Tractive Effort* is quoted which represents the current which the equipment can take continuously.

3. The power of its engine. Not all power reaches the rail, as electrical machines are approximately 90% efficient. As the electrical energy passes through two such machines (the generator or alternator and the traction motors), the *Power at Rail* is approximately 81% (90% of 90%) of the engine power, less a further amount used for auxiliary equipment such as radiator fans, traction motor blowers, air compressors, battery charging, cab heating, Electric Train Supply (ETS) etc. The power of the locomotive is proportional to the tractive effort times the speed. Hence when on full power there is a speed corresponding to the continuous tractive effort.

HAULAGE CAPABILITY OF ELECTRIC LOCOMOTIVES

Unlike a diesel locomotive, an electric locomotive does not develop its power on board and its performance is determined only by two factors, namely its weight and the characteristics of its electrical equipment. Whereas a diesel locomotive tends to be a constant power machine, the power of an electric locomotive varies considerably. Up to a certain speed it can produce virtually a constant tractive effort. Hence power rises with speed according to the formula given in section three above, until a maximum speed is reached at which tractive effort falls, such that the power also falls. Hence the power at the speed corresponding to the maximum tractive effort is lower than the maximum speed.

BRAKE FORCE

Brake Force (also known as brake power) is a measure of the braking power of a locomotive. The Brake Force available is dependant on the adhesion between the rail and the wheels being braked and the normal reaction of the rail on the wheels being braked (and hence on the weight per braked wheel). A locomotive's Brake Force is shown on its data panels so operating staff can ensure sufficient brake power is available for specific trains.

ELECTRIC TRAIN SUPPLY (ETS)

A number of locomotives are equipped to provide a supply of electricity to the train being hauled to power auxiliaries such as heating, cooling fans, air conditioning and kitchen equipment. ETS is provided from the locomotive by means of a separate alternator (except Class 33 locomotives, which have a DC generator). The ETS index of a locomotive is a measure of the electrical power available for train supply. Class 55 locomotives provide an ETS directly from one of their traction generators into the train supply.

Similarly, most locomotive-hauled carriages also have an ETS index, which in this case is a measure of the power required to operate equipment mounted in the carriage. The sum of the ETS indices of all the hauled vehicles in a train must not exceed the ETS index of the locomotive.

ETS is commonly (but incorrectly) known as ETH (Electric Train Heating), which is a throwback to the days before locomotive-hauled carriages were equipped with electrically powered auxiliary equipment other than for train heating.

ROUTE AVAILABILITY (RA)

This is a measure of a railway vehicle's axle load. The higher the axle load of a vehicle, the higher the RA number on a scale from 1 to 10. Each Network Rail route has a RA number and in general no vehicle with a higher RA number may travel on that route without special clearance.

MULTIPLE WORKING

Multiple working between vehicles (ie two or more powered vehicles being driven from one cab) is facilitated by jumper cables connecting the vehicles. However, not all types of locomotive are compatible with each other, and a number of different systems are in use. Some are compatible with others, some are not. BR used "multiple working codes" to designate which locomotives were compatible. The list below shows which classes of locomotives are compatible with each other – the former BR multiple working code being shown in brackets. It should be noted that some locomotives have had the equipment removed or made inoperable.

With other classes:
Classes 20, 25, 31, 33, 37 40 & 73/1*. (Blue Star)
Classes 56 & 58. (Red Diamond)
Classes 59, 66, 67, 68, 70, 73/9 & 88.
* DRS has since adapted the systems so its Classes 20/3, 37 & 57 can work with each other only.

With other members of same class only:
Class 43, Class 47 (Green Circle), Class 50 (Orange Square), Class 60.

PUSH-PULL OPERATION

Some locomotives are modified to operate passenger and service (formed of laboratory, test and inspection carriages) trains in "push-pull" mode – which allows the train to be driven from either end – either with locomotives at each end (both under power) or with a driving brake van at one end and a locomotive at the other. Various different systems are now in use. Electric locomotive Classes 86, 87, 90 & 91 use a time-division multiplex (TDM) system for push-pull working which utilises the existing Railway Clearing House (RCH) jumper cables fitted to carriages. Previously these cables had only been used to control train lighting and public address systems.

More recently locomotives of Classes 67 and 68 have used the Association of American Railroads (AAR) system.

ABBREVIATIONS

Standard abbreviations used in this section of the book are:

a	Train air brake equipment only.
b	Drophead buckeye couplers.
c	Scharfenberg couplers.
d	Fitted with retractable Dellner couplers.
e	European Railway Traffic Management System (ERTMS) signalling equipment fitted.
k	Fitted with Swinghead Automatic "buckeye" combination couplers.
p	Train air, vacuum and electro-pneumatic brakes.
r	Radio Electric Token Block signalling equipment fitted.
s	Slow Speed Control equipment.
v	Train vacuum brake only.
x	Train air and vacuum brakes ("Dual brakes").
+	Additional fuel tank capacity.
§	Sandite laying equipment.

In all cases use of the above abbreviations indicates the equipment in question is normally operable. The definition of non-standard abbreviations and symbols is detailed in individual class headings.

1.1. DIESEL SHUNTING LOCOMOTIVES

All BR design shunting locomotives still in existence, apart from those considered to be preserved, are listed together in this section. Preserved shunting locomotives are listed in the Platform 5 publication "Preserved Locomotives of British Railways" (a small number are listed in both that book and in this publication).

Few shunting locomotives have engineering acceptance and are equipped to operate on Network Rail infrastructure (beyond interface infrastructure), but those that are known to be permitted are indicated here.

For shunting locomotives, instead of the two-letter depot code, actual locations at the time of publication are given. Pool codes for shunting locomotives are not shown.

CLASS 03   BR/GARDNER   0-6-0

Built: 1958–62 by BR at Swindon or Doncaster Works.
Engine: Gardner 8L3 of 152 kW (204 hp) at 1200 rpm.
Transmission: Mechanical. Fluidrive type 23 hydraulic coupling to Wilson-Drewry CA5R7 gearbox with SCG type RF11 final drive.
Maximum Tractive Effort: 68 kN (15300 lbf).
Continuous Tractive Effort: 68 kN (15300 lbf) at 3.75 mph.
Train Brakes: Air & vacuum.
Brake Force: 13 t.   **Dimensions:** 7.93 x 2.59 m.
Weight: 31.3 t.   **Wheel Diameter:** 1092 mm.
Design Speed: 28.5 mph.   **Maximum Speed:** 28.5 mph.
Fuel Capacity: 1364 litres.   **Route Availability:** 1.
Train Supply: Not equipped.   **Total:** 3.

Number	Notes	Livery	Owner	Location
03084	**G**	WC	West Coast Railway Company, Carnforth Depot
03196	**B**	WC	West Coast Railway Company, Carnforth Depot
D2381	v **G**	WC	West Coast Railway Company, Carnforth Depot

CLASS 07   BR/RUSTON & HORNSBY   0-6-0

Built: 1962 by Ruston & Hornsby, Lincoln.
Engine: Paxman 6RPHL Mk III of 205 kW (275 hp) at 1360 rpm.
Transmission: Electric. One AEI RTB 6652 traction motor.
Maximum Tractive Effort: 126 kN (28240 lbf).
Continuous Tractive Effort: 71 kN (15950 lbf) at 4.38 mph.
Train Brakes: Vacuum.
Brake Force: **Dimensions:** 8.17 x 2.59 m.
Weight: 43.6 t.   **Wheel Diameter:** 1067 mm.
Design Speed: 20 mph.   **Maximum Speed:** 20 mph.
Fuel Capacity: 1400 litres.   **Train Supply:** Not equipped.
Total: 1.

07007	v **B**	AF	Arlington Fleet Services, Eastleigh Works, Hants

CLASS 08   BR/ENGLISH ELECTRIC   0-6-0

Built: 1955–62 by BR at Crewe, Darlington, Derby Locomotive, Doncaster or Horwich Works.
Engine: English Electric 6KT of 298 kW (400 hp) at 680 rpm.
Main Generator: English Electric 801.
Traction Motors: Two English Electric 506.
Maximum Tractive Effort: 156 kN (35000 lbf).
Continuous Tractive Effort: 49 kN (11100 lbf) at 8.8 mph.

Power at Rail: 194 kW (260 hp).	**Train Brakes:** Air & vacuum.
Brake Force: 19 t.	**Dimensions:** 8.92 x 2.59 m.
Weight: 49.6–50.4 t.	**Wheel Diameter:** 1372 mm.
Design Speed: 20 mph.	**Maximum Speed:** 15 mph.
Fuel Capacity: 3037 litres.	**Route Availability:** 5.
Train Supply: Not equipped.	**Total:** 170.

* Locomotives with engineering acceptance to operate on Network Rail infrastructure. 08850 has acceptance for use between Battersby and Whitby only, for rescue purposes.

† – Fitted with remote control equipment.

Non-standard liveries:

08308	All over ScotRail Caledonian Sleeper purple.
08401	Dark green.
08423	Dark blue.
08442	Dark grey lower bodyside & light grey upper bodyside.
08445	Yellow, blue & green.
08447	Lilac.
08502	Mid blue.
08568	Dark grey lower bodyside & light grey upper bodyside. Red solebar stripe.
08598	Yellow.
08600	Red with a light grey roof.
08630	Black with red cabsides and solebar stripe.
08645	All over black with a white cross.
08682	Multi-coloured.
08730	ABP Ports blue
08774	Red with a light grey roof.
08870	Light grey.
08899	Crimson lake.
08956	Serco Railtest green.

Number	Notes	Livery	Owner	Location
08220	v	**B**	EE	Nottingham Transport Heritage Centre, Ruddington
08308	a	**0**	RL	Weardale Railway, Wolsingham, County Durham
08331		**K**	20	Midland Railway-Butterley, Derbyshire
08375	a	**RL**	RL	Victoria Group, Port of Boston, Boston
08389	a†	**E**	HN	Celsa Steel UK, Tremorfa Steelworks, Cardiff
08401	a	**0**	HU	LH Group, Barton-under-Needwood, Staffordshire (S)
08405	a†	**E**	RS	East Midlands Railway, Neville Hill Depot, Leeds
08410	* a	**GW**	AD	AV Dawson, Ayrton Rail Terminal, Middlesbrough
08411	a	**B**	RS	RSS, Rye Farm, Wishaw, Sutton Coldfield (S)

08417	* a	Y	NR	Loram (UK), RTC Business Park, Derby
08418	a	E	WC	West Coast Railway Company, Carnforth Depot
08423	a	0	RL	PD Ports, Teesport, Grangetown, Middlesbrough
08428	ak	E	HN	Barrow Hill Roundhouse, Chesterfield, Derbys (S)
08441	* a	RS	RS	Hitachi, Bounds Green Depot, London
08442	a	0	AV	Arriva TrainCare, Eastleigh Depot, Hampshire (S)
08445	a	0	HU	Daventry International Railfreight Terminal, Crick
08447	a	0	RU	John G Russell (Transport), Hillington, Glasgow (S)
08451	*	B	AM	Alstom, Longsight Depot, Manchester
08454	*	B	AM	Alstom, Widnes Technology Centre, Merseyside
08460	a	RS	RS	GB Railfreight, Eastleigh East Yard
08472	* a	WA	WA	Hitachi, Craigentinny Depot, Edinburgh
08480	* a	RS	RS	Arriva TrainCare, Bristol Barton Hill Depot
08483	* a	K	LS	L&NWR Heritage Company, Crewe Diesel Depot
08484	a	RS	RS	Greater Anglia, Crown Point Depot, Norwich
08485	a	B	WC	West Coast Railway Company, Carnforth Depot
08499	a	B	CS	Colas Rail, Canton Depot, Cardiff
08500		E	HN	Nemesis Rail, Burton-upon-Trent, Staffordshire (S)
08502		0	HN	East Kent Light Railway, Shepherdswell, Kent (S)
08507	a	RB	RV	Arlington Fleet Services, Eastleigh Works
08511	a	RS	RS	GB Railfreight, Eastleigh East Yard
08516	a	LW	RS	RSS, Rye Farm, Wishaw, Sutton Coldfield
08523	*	B	RL	Weardale Railway, Wolsingham, County Durham
08525		ST	EM	East Midlands Railway, Neville Hill Depot, Leeds (S)
08527		FA	HN	Attero Recycling, Rossington, Doncaster
08530	*	FL	FL	Freightliner, Trafford Park FLT
08531	* a	FH	FL	Freightliner, Felixstowe FLT
08536		B	RS	RSS, Rye Farm, Wishaw, Sutton Coldfield (S)
08567		E	AF	Arlington Fleet Services, Eastleigh Works, Hants
08568		0	RS	RSS, Rye Farm, Wishaw, Sutton Coldfield (S)
08571	* a	WA	WA	Daventry International Railfreight Terminal, Crick
08573		K	RL	Weardale Railway, Wolsingham, County Durham
08575		FL	FL	Nemesis Rail, Burton-upon-Trent, Staffordshire (S)
08578		E	HN	Quinton Rail Technology Centre, Long Marston, Warks (S)
08580	*	RS	RS	Hitachi, Bounds Green Depot, London
08585	*	FH	FL	Freightliner, Southampton Maritime FLT
08588		RL	RL	Loram (UK), RTC Business Park, Derby
08593		E	RS	RSS, Rye Farm, Wishaw, Sutton Coldfield (S)
08596	* a†	WA	WA	Hitachi, Craigentinny Depot, Edinburgh
08598		0	AD	RSS, Rye Farm, Wishaw, Sutton Coldfield
08600	a	0	AD	AV Dawson, Ayrton Rail Terminal, Middlesbrough
08602		B	BT	Bombardier Transportation, Derby Works (S)
08605	†	DB	RV	Ecclesbourne Valley Railway, Wirksworth, Derbyshire
08611	*	B	AM	Alstom, Wembley Depot, London
08613		RL	RL	Weardale Railway, Wolsingham, County Durham
08615	*	HU	WA	Tata Steel, Shotton Works, Deeside
08616		LM	WM	West Midlands Trains, Tyseley Depot, Birmingham
08617	*	B	AM	Alstom, Oxley Depot, Wolverhampton
08622		K	RL	Hanson Cement, Ketton Cement Works, nr Stamford
08623		DB	HN	Breedon, Hope Cement Works, Derbys (S)
08624	*	FH	FL	Freightliner, Southampton Maritime FLT

08630	†	**K**	HN	Celsa Steel UK, Tremorfa Steelworks, Cardiff
08631		**B**	LS	Weardale Railway, Wolsingham, County Durham
08632	†	**RS**	RS	Loram (UK), RTC Business Park, Derby
08641	*	**B**	GW	Great Western Railway, Laira Depot, Plymouth
08643		**B**	MR	Aggregate Industries, Merehead Rail Terminal
08644	*	**B**	GW	Great Western Railway, Laira Depot, Plymouth
08645	*	**O**	GW	Great Western Railway, Long Rock Depot, Penzance
08648	*	**K**	RL	ScotRail, Inverness Depot
08649		**KB**	ME	Meteor Power, Silverstone
08650		**B**	MR	RSS, Rye Farm, Wishaw, Sutton Coldfield
08652		**B**	RS	RSS, Rye Farm, Wishaw, Sutton Coldfield (S)
08653		**E**	HN	Quinton Rail Technology Centre, Long Marston, Warks (S)
08663	* a	**B**	HH	Chrysalis Rail, Landore Depot, Swansea
08669	* a	**WA**	WA	Wabtec Rail, Doncaster Works
08670	* a	**RS**	RS	GB Railfreight, Bescot Yard
08676		**E**	HN	East Kent Light Railway, Shepherdswell, Kent (S)
08678	a	**WC**	WC	West Coast Railway Company, Carnforth Depot
08682		**O**	BT	Bombardier Transportation, Derby Works (S)
08683	*	**RS**	RS	Greater Anglia, Crown Point Depot, Norwich
08685		**E**	HN	East Kent Light Railway, Shepherdswell, Kent (S)
08690		**ST**	EM	East Midlands Railway, Neville Hill Depot, Leeds (S)
08691	*	**FL**	FL	Freightliner, Crewe Basford Hall Yard, Cheshire
08696	* a	**B**	AM	Alstom, Wembley Depot, London
08700		**B**	RL	Bombardier Transportation, Ilford Works, London
08701	a	**RX**	HN	Quinton Rail Technology Centre, Long Marston, Warks (S)
08703	a	**E**	RS	DB Cargo UK, Springs Branch Depot, Wigan
08704		**RB**	RV	Ecclesbourne Valley Railway, Wirksworth, Derbys
08706	†	**E**	HN	RSS, Rye Farm, Wishaw, Sutton Coldfield (S)
08709		**E**	RS	RSS, Rye Farm, Wishaw, Sutton Coldfield (S)
08711	k	**RX**	HN	Nemesis Rail, Burton-upon-Trent, Staffordshire (S)
08714		**E**	HN	Breedon, Hope Cement Works, Derbys (S)
08721	*	**B**	AM	Alstom, Widnes Technology Centre, Merseyside
08724	*	**WA**	WA	Wabtec Rail, Doncaster Works
08730		**O**	RS	RSS, Rye Farm, Wishaw, Sutton Coldfield
08735	†	**AW**	AV	Arriva TrainCare, Eastleigh Depot
08737		**G**	LS	L&NWR Heritage Company, Crewe Diesel Depot
08738		**RS**	RS	Felixstowe FLT
08742	†	**RX**	HN	Barrow HIll Roundhouse, Chesterfield, Derbys (S)
08743		**B**	SU	SembCorp Utilities UK, Wilton, Middlesbrough
08752	†	**RS**	RS	Gemini Rail Group, Wolverton Works, Milton Keynes
08754	*	**B**	RL	Weardale Railway, Wolsingham, County Durham
08756		**DG**	RL	Weardale Railway, Wolsingham, County Durham
08757		**RG**	PO	Telford Steam Railway, Shropshire
08762		**RL**	RL	Eastern Rail Services, Great Yarmouth
08764	*	**B**	AM	Alstom, Polmadie Depot, Glasgow
08765		**HN**	HN	Barrow Hill Roundhouse, Chesterfield, Derbys (S)
08774	a	**O**	AD	AV Dawson, Ayrton Rail Terminal, Middlesbrough
08780		**G**	LS	L&NWR Heritage Company, Crewe Diesel Depot
08782	a†	**CU**	HN	Barrow HIll Roundhouse, Chesterfield, Derbys (S)
08783		**E**	EY	European Metal Recycling, Kingsbury, nr Tamworth
08784		**DG**	PO	EMD, Longport Works, Stoke-on-Trent

08785	* a	FL	FL	Freightliner, Southampton FLT
08786	a	DG	HN	Barrow Hill Roundhouse, Chesterfield, Derbys (S)
08787		B	MR	Hanson Aggregates, Whatley Quarry, near Frome
08788	*	RL	RL	PD Ports, Teesport, Grangetown, Middlesbrough
08790	*	B	AM	Alstom, Edge Hill Depot, Liverpool
08798		E	HN	Barrow Hill Roundhouse, Chesterfield, Derbys (S)
08799	a	E	HN	East Kent Light Railway, Shepherdswell, Kent (S)
08802	†	E	HN	RSS, Rye Farm, Wishaw, Sutton Coldfield (S)
08804	†	E	HN	East Kent Light Railway, Shepherdswell, Kent (S)
08805		FO	WM	West Midlands Trains, Soho Depot, Birmingham
08809		RL	RL	Hanson Cement, Ketton Cement Works, nr Stamford
08810	a	LW	AV	Arriva TrainCare, Eastleigh Depot, Hampshire
08818		GB	HN	HNRC, Worksop Depot, Nottinghamshire
08822	*	IC	GW	Great Western Railway, St Philip's Marsh Depot, Bristol
08823	a	HU	HU	Tata Steel, Shotton Works, Deeside
08824	ak	K	HN	Barrow Hill Roundhouse, Chesterfield, Derbys (S)
08834		HN	HN	Northern, Allerton Depot, Liverpool
08836	*	GW	GW	Great Western Railway, Reading Depot
08846		B	RS	East Midlands Railway, Neville Hill Depot, Leeds
08847	*	CD	RL	PD Ports, Teesport, Grangetown, Middlesbrough
08850	*	B	NY	North Yorkshire Moors Railway, Grosmont Depot
08853	* a	WA	WA	Wabtec Rail, Doncaster Works
08865		E	HN	Bombardier Transportation, Central Rivers Depot, Barton-under-Needwood
08868		AW	HN	Arriva TrainCare, Crewe Depot, Cheshire
08870		O	RL	Weardale Railway, Wolsingham, County Durham
08871		CD	RL	Bombardier Transportation, Ilford Works, London
08872		E	HN	European Metal Recycling, Attercliffe, Sheffield (S)
08873	*	RX	HU	LH Group, Barton-under-Needwood, Staffordshire (S)
08874	*	SL	RL	Weardale Railway, Wolsingham, County Durham
08877		DG	HN	Celsa Steel UK, Tremorfa Steelworks, Cardiff
08879		E	HN	Breedon, Hope Cement Works, Derbys (S)
08885		B	RL	Weardale Railway, Wolsingham, County Durham (S)
08887	* a	B	AM	Alstom, Polmadie Depot, Glasgow
08891	*	FL	HN	LH Group, Barton-under-Needwood, Staffordshire (S)
08892		DR	HN	Bombardier Transportation, Old Dalby Test Centre, Asfordby
08899		O	EM	East Midlands Railway, Derby Etches Park Depot
08903		B	SU	SembCorp Utilities UK, Wilton, Middlesbrough
08904	d	E	HN	HNRC, Worksop Depot, Nottinghamshire
08905		E	HN	Breedon, Hope Cement Works, Derbys (S)
08908		ST	EM	East Midlands Railway, Neville Hill Depot, Leeds (S)
08912		B	AD	AV Dawson, Ayrton Rail Terminal, Middlesbrough (S)
08918		DG	HN	Nemesis Rail, Burton-upon-Trent, Staffordshire (S)
08921		E	RS	RSS, Rye Farm, Wishaw, Sutton Coldfield (S)
08922		DG	PO	Hitachi Rail Europe, Newton Aycliffe, Co Durham
08924	†	GB	HN	Celsa Steel UK, Tremorfa Steelworks, Cardiff
08925		G	GB	GB Railfreight, Whitemoor Yard, March, Cambs
08927		G	RS	GB Railfreight, Bescot Yard
08933		B	MR	Aggregate Industries, Merehead Rail Terminal
08934	a	VP	GB	GB Railfreight, Whitemoor Yard, March, Cambs
08936		B	RL	Weardale Railway, Wolsingham, County Durham

08937		G	BD	Dartmoor Railway, Meldon Quarry, nr Okehampton
08939		**ECR**	RS	Chasewater Railway, Staffordshire
08943		**HN**	HN	Barrow HIll Roundhouse, Chesterfield, Derbys
08947		**B**	MR	Hanson Aggregates, Whatley Quarry, near Frome
08948	c	**EP**	EU	Eurostar, Temple Mills Depot, London
08950		**ST**	EM	East Midlands Railway, Neville Hill Depot, Leeds (S)
08954	*	**B**	AM	Alstom, Longsight Depot, Manchester
08956		**O**	LO	Bombardier Transportation, Old Dalby Test Centre, Asfordby

Class 08/9. Reduced height cab. Converted 1985–87 by BR at Landore.

| 08994 | a | **E** | HN | Nemesis Rail, Burton-upon-Trent, Staffordshire (S) |

Other numbers or names carried:

08308	"23"	08737	D3905
08423	"H011" / "14"	08743	Bryan Turner
08451	LONGSIGHT TMD	08754	"H041"
08460	SPIRIT OF THE OAK	08757	EAGLE C.U.R.C.
08483	Bungle	08762	"H067"
08484	CAPTAIN NATHANIEL DARELL	08774	ARTHUR VERNON DAWSON
08499	REDLIGHT	08780	Zippy / D3948
08525	DUNCAN BEDFORD	08787	"08296"
08568	St. Rollox	08790	M.A. SMITH
08585	Vicky	08805	Robin Jones
08588	"H047"		40 YEARS SERVICE
08602	"004"	08809	"24"
08605	G.R. Walker	08810	RICHARD J. WENHAM
08613	"H064"		EASTLEIGH DEPOT
08615	UNCLE DAI		DECEMBER 1989 – JULY 1999
08616	TYSELEY 100 / 3783	08818	MOLLY / "4"
08617	Steve Purser	08822	Dave Mills
08622	"H028" / "19"	08823	KEVLA
08624	Rambo PAUL RAMSEY	08824	"IEMD 01"
08629	Wolverton	08846	"003"
08630	"CELSA 3"	08865	GILLY
08641	Pride of Laira	08870	"H024"
08644	Laira Diesel Depot	08871	"H074"
	50 Years 1962–2012	08885	"H042" / "18"
08645	St. Piran	08899	Midland Counties Railway
08649	Bradwell		175 1839–2014
08669	Bob Machin	08903	John W Antill
08678	"555"	08924	"CELSA 2"
08682	Lionheart	08927	D4157
08690	DAVID THIRKILL	08934	D4164
08691	Terri	08937	D4167
08735	Geoff Hobbs 42	08950	DAVID LIGHTFOOT

CLASS 09   BR/ENGLISH ELECTRIC   0-6-0

Built: 1959–62 by BR at Darlington or Horwich Works.
Engine: English Electric 6KT of 298 kW (400 hp) at 680 rpm.
Main Generator: English Electric 801.
Traction Motors: English Electric 506.
Maximum Tractive Effort: 111 kN (25000 lbf).
Continuous Tractive Effort: 39 kN (8800 lbf) at 11.6 mph.

Power at Rail: 201 kW (269 hp).	**Train Brakes:** Air & vacuum.
Brake Force: 19 t.	**Dimensions:** 8.92 x 2.59 m.
Weight: 49 t.	**Wheel Diameter:** 1372 mm.
Design Speed: 27 mph.	**Maximum Speed:** 27 mph.
Fuel Capacity: 3037 litres.	**Route Availability:** 5.
Train Supply: Not equipped.	**Total:** 10.

Class 09/0. Built as Class 09.

09002	**G**	GB	GB Railfreight, Whitemoor Yard, March, Cambs
09006	**E**	HN	Nemesis Rail, Burton-upon-Trent, Staffordshire (S)
09007	**G**	LN	London Overground, Willesden Depot, London
09009	**G**	GB	Miles Platting Stone Terminal, Greater Manchester
09014	**DG**	HN	Nemesis Rail, Burton-upon-Trent, Staffordshire (S)
09022	**B**	VG	Victoria Group, Port of Boston, Boston
09023	**E**	EY	European Metal Recycling, Attercliffe, Sheffield (S)

Class 09/1. Converted from Class 08 1992–93 by RFS Industries, Kilnhurst.
110 V electrical equipment.

09106	**HN**	HN	Celsa Steel UK, Tremorfa Steelworks, Cardiff

Class 09/2. Converted from Class 08 1992 by RFS Industries, Kilnhurst.
90 V electrical equipment.

09201	**DG**	HN	Breedon, Hope Cement Works, Derbys (S)
09204	**AW**	AV	Arriva TrainCare, Crewe Depot, Cheshire

Other numbers or names carried:

09007	D3671
09106	"6"

1.2. MAIN LINE DIESEL LOCOMOTIVES

CLASS 19

Experimental locomotive being rebuilt by Artemis Intelligent Power from a Mark 3B Driving Brake Van. Part of a project funded by the Rail Safety & Standards Board (RSSB) to test the viability of combining hydrostatic transmission to reduce engine emissions. Conversion work is taking place at the Bo'ness & Kinneil Railway. Full details awaited.

Built: 1988 by BR Derby Works.
Engine: 2 x JCB diesel engines.
Main Generator:
Traction Motors:
Maximum Tractive Effort:
Continuous Tractive Effort: **Train Brakes:**
Power at Rail: **Dimensions:** 18.83 x 2.71 m.
Brake Force: **Weight:**
Design Speed: **Maximum Speed:**
Fuel Capacity: **Route Availability:**
Train Supply: **Total:** 1.

19001	(82113)	**B**	AV	BO

CLASS 20   ENGLISH ELECTRIC   Bo-Bo

Built: 1957–68 by English Electric at Vulcan Foundry, Newton-le-Willows or by Robert Stephenson & Hawthorns at Darlington.
Engine: English Electric 8SVT Mk II of 746 kW (1000 hp) at 850 rpm.
Main Generator: English Electric 819/3C.
Traction Motors: English Electric 526/5D or 526/8D.
Maximum Tractive Effort: 187 kN (42000 lbf).
Continuous Tractive Effort: 111 kN (25000 lbf) at 11 mph.
Power at Rail: 574 kW (770 hp).   **Train Brakes:** Air & vacuum.
Brake Force: 35 t.   **Dimensions:** 14.25 x 2.67 m.
Weight: 73.4–73.5 t.   **Wheel Diameter:** 1092 mm.
Design Speed: 75 mph.   **Maximum Speed:** 75 mph.
Fuel Capacity: 1727 litres.   **Route Availability:** 5.
Train Supply: Not equipped.   **Total:** 32.

Non-standard liveries/numbering:

20056	Yellow with grey cabsides and red solebar. Carries No. "81".
20066	Dark blue with yellow stripes. Carries No. "82".
20096	Carries original number D8096.
20107	Carries original number D8107.
20110	Carries original number D8110.
20142	LUL Maroon.
20168	White with green cabsides and solebar. Carries No. "2".
20227	LUL Maroon.
20906	White. Carries No. "3".

Class 20/0. Standard Design.

20007	**G**	EE	MOLO	SK	
20056	**O**	HN	HNRL	SC (S)	
20066	**O**	HN	HNRL	HO	
20096	**G**	LS	LSLO	CL	
20107	**G**	LS	LSLO	CL	
20110	**G**	HN	HNRS	WS (S)	
20118	**FO**	HN	GBEE	WS	Saltburn-by-the-Sea
20121	**HN**	HN	HNRL	BH (S)	
20132	**FO**	HN	GBEE	WS	Barrow Hill Depot
20142	**O**	20	MOLO	SK	SIR JOHN BETJEMAN
20168	**O**	HN	HNRL	HO	SIR GEORGE EARLE
20189	**B**	20	MOLO	SK	
20205	**B**	2L	MOLO	SK	
20227	**O**	2L	MOLO	SK	SHERLOCK HOLMES

Class 20/3. Direct Rail Services refurbished locomotives. Details as Class 20/0 except:

Refurbished: 15 locomotives were refurbished 1995–96 by Brush Traction at Loughborough (20301–305) or 1997–98 by RFS(E) at Doncaster (20306–315). Disc indicators or headcode panels removed.

Train Brakes: Air.   **Maximum Speed:** 60 mph (+ 75 mph).
Weight: 73 t (+ 76 t).   **Fuel Capacity:** 2909 (+ 4909) litres.
Brake Force: 35 t (+ 31 t).   **RA:** 5 (+ 6).

20301	(20047) r	**DS**	DR	XHSS	BH (S)
20302	(20084) r	**DS**	DR	XHSS	BO (S)
20303	(20127) r	**DS**	DR	XHSS	ZR (S)	Max Joule 1958–1999
20304	(20120) r	**DS**	DR	XHHP	BH (S)
20305	(20095) r	**DS**	DR	XHSS	BO (S)
20308	(20187) r+	**DS**	DR	XHHP	BH (S)
20309	(20075) r+	**DS**	DR	XHHP	BH (S)
20311	(20102) r+	**HN**	HN	HNRL	BH
20312	(20042) r+	**DS**	DR	XHHP	BH (S)
20314	(20117) r+	**HN**	HN	HNRL	BH

Class 20/9. Harry Needle Railroad Company (former Hunslet-Barclay/ DRS) locomotives. Details as Class 20/0 except:

Refurbished: 1989 by Hunslet-Barclay at Kilmarnock.
Train Brakes: Air.   **Fuel Capacity:** 1727 (+ 4727) litres.
RA: 5 (+ 6).

20901	(20101)	**GB**	HN	GBEE	WS
20903	(20083) +	**DR**	HN	HNRS	BU (S)
20904	(20041)	**DR**	HN	HNRS	BU (S)
20905	(20225) +	**GB**	HN	GBEE	BH	Dave Darwin
20906	(20219)	**O**	HN	HNRL	HO

CLASS 25   BR/BEYER PEACOCK/SULZER   Bo-Bo

Built: 1965 by Beyer Peacock at Gorton.
Engine: Sulzer 6LDA28-B of 930 kW (1250 hp) at 750 rpm.
Main Generator: AEI RTB15656.   **Traction Motors:** AEI 253AY.
Maximum Tractive Effort: 200 kN (45000 lbf).
Continuous Tractive Effort: 93 kN (20800 lbf) at 17.1 mph.
Power at Rail: 708 kW (949 hp).   **Train Brakes:** Air & vacuum.
Brake Force: 38 t.   **Dimensions:** 15.39 x 2.73 m.
Weight: 71.5 t.   **Wheel Diameter:** 1143 mm.
Design Speed: 90 mph.   **Maximum Speed:** 60 mph.
Fuel Capacity: 2270 litres.   **Route Availability:** 5.
Train Supply: Not equipped.   **Total:** 1.

Carries original number D7628.

Only certified for use on Network Rail tracks between Whitby and Battersby, as an extension of North Yorkshire Moors Railway services.

25278	**GG**	NY	MBDL	NY	SYBILLA

CLASS 31   BRUSH/ENGLISH ELECTRIC   A1A-A1A

Built: 1958–62 by Brush Traction at Loughborough.
Engine: English Electric 12SVT of 1100 kW (1470 hp) at 850 rpm.
Main Generator: Brush TG160-48.   **Traction Motors:** Brush TM73-68.
Maximum Tractive Effort: 160 kN (35900 lbf).
Continuous Tractive Effort: 83 kN (18700 lbf) at 23.5 mph.
Power at Rail: 872 kW (1170 hp).   **Train Brakes:** Air & vacuum.
Brake Force: 49 t.   **Dimensions:** 17.30 x 2.67 m.
Weight: 106.7–111 t.   **Wheel Diameter:** 1092/1003 mm.
Design Speed: 90 mph.   **Maximum Speed:** 90 mph.
Fuel Capacity: 2409 litres.   **Route Availability:** 5.
Train Supply: Not equipped.   **Total:** 1.

31128	**B**	NS	NRLO	BU	CHARYBDIS

CLASS 33   BRCW/SULZER   Bo-Bo

Built: 1959–62 by the Birmingham Railway Carriage & Wagon Company at Smethwick.
Engine: Sulzer 8LDA28 of 1160 kW (1550 hp) at 750 rpm.
Main Generator: Crompton Parkinson CG391B1.
Traction Motors: Crompton Parkinson C171C2.
Maximum Tractive Effort: 200 kN (45000 lbf).
Continuous Tractive Effort: 116 kN (26000 lbf) at 17.5 mph.
Power at Rail: 906 kW (1215 hp).   **Train Brakes:** Air & vacuum.
Brake Force: 35 t.   **Dimensions:** 15.47 x 2.82 (2.64 m 33/2).
Weight: 76-78 t.   **Wheel Diameter:** 1092 mm.
Design Speed: 85 mph.   **Maximum Speed:** 85 mph.

Fuel Capacity: 3410 litres.   **Route Availability:** 6.
Train Supply: Electric, index 48 (750 V DC only).
Total: 5.

Non-standard numbering: 33012 Carries original number D6515.

Class 33/0. Standard Design.

33012	**G**	71	MBDL	SW	Lt Jenny Lewis RN
33025	**WC**	WC	AWCA	CS	
33029	**WC**	WC	AWCA	CS	
33030	**DR**	WC	AWCX	CS (S)	

Class 33/2. Built to former Loading Gauge of Tonbridge–Battle Line.
Equipped with slow speed control.

33207	**WC**	WC	AWCA	CS	Jim Martin

CLASS 37   ENGLISH ELECTRIC   Co-Co

Built: 1960–66 by English Electric at Vulcan Foundry, Newton-le-Willows or by Robert Stephenson & Hawthorns at Darlington.
Engine: English Electric 12CSVT of 1300 kW (1750 hp) at 850 rpm.
Main Generator: English Electric 822/10G.
Traction Motors: English Electric 538/A.
Maximum Tractive Effort: 247 kN (55500 lbf).
Continuous Tractive Effort: 156 kN (35000 lbf) at 13.6 mph.
Power at Rail: 932 kW (1250 hp).   **Train Brakes:** Air & vacuum.
Brake Force: 50 t.   **Dimensions:** 18.75 x 2.74 m.
Weight: 102.8–108.4 t.   **Wheel Diameter:** 1092 mm.
Design Speed: 90 mph.   **Maximum Speed:** 80 mph.
Fuel Capacity: 4046 (+ 7683) litres. **Route Availability:** 5 (§ 6).
Train Supply: Not equipped.   **Total:** 66.

Non-standard numbering:

37424 Also carries the number 37558.
37521 Carries original number D6817.
37667 Carries original number D6851.
37703 Carries the number 37067.
37905 Also carries original number D6838.

Class 37/0. Standard Design.

37025	**BL**	37	COTS	NM	Inverness TMD
37038 a	**DI**	DR	XHNC	KM	
37057	**CS**	CS	COTS	NM	
37059 ar+	**DI**	DR	XHNC	KM	
37069 ar+	**DI**	DR	XHNC	KM	
37099	**CS**	CS	COTS	NM	MERL EVANS 1947–2016
37116 +	**CS**	CS	COTS	NM	
37146	**CE**	EP	EPUK	LR (S)	
37165 a+	**CE**	WC	AWCX	CS (S)	
37175 a	**CS**	CS	COTS	NM	
37190	**B**	LS	MBDL	CL	

37198 +	Y	NR	MBDL	ZA (S)	
37207	B	EP	MBDL	LR (S)	
37218 ar+	DI	DR	XHNC	KM	
37219	CS	CS	COTS	NM	Jonty Jarvis 8-12-1998 to 18-3-2005
37240	F	NB	COFS	NM	
37254	CS	CS	COTS	NM	Cardiff Canton
37259 ar	DS	DR	XHSS	KM (S)	

Class 37/4. Refurbished with electric train supply equipment. Main generator replaced by alternator. Regeared (CP7) bogies. Details as Class 37/0 except:
Main Alternator: Brush BA1005A.   **Power At Rail:** 935 kW (1254 hp).
Traction Motors: English Electric 538/5A.
Maximum Tractive Effort: 256 kN (57440 lbf).
Continuous Tractive Effort: 184 kN (41250 lbf) at 11.4 mph.
Weight: 107 t.   **Design Speed:** 80 mph.
Fuel Capacity: 7683 litres.
Train Supply: Electric, index 30.

37401 ar	BL	DR	XHAC	KM	Mary Queen of Scots
37402 a	BL	DR	XHAC	KM	Stephen Middlemore 23.12.1954–8.6.2013
37403	BL	SP	RAJV	BO	Isle of Mull
37405 ar	DS	DR	XHAC	KM	
37407	BL	DR	XHAC	KM	Blackpool Tower
37409 ar	BL	DR	XHSS	KM (S)	Lord Hinton
37418	BL	SB	COTS	NM	An Comunn Gaidhealach
37419 ar	IC	DR	XHAC	KM	Carl Haviland 1954–2012
37421	CS	CS	COTS	NM	
37422 ar	DR	DR	XHAC	KM	
37423 ar	DR	DR	XHAC	KM	Spirit of the Lakes
37424	BL	DR	XHAC	KM	Avro Vulcan XH558
37425 ar	RR	DR	XHAC	KM	Sir Robert McAlpine/Concrete Bob

Class 37/5. Refurbished without train supply equipment. Main generator replaced by alternator. Regeared (CP7) bogies. Details as Class 37/4 except:
Power At Rail: 932 kW (1250 hp).
Maximum Tractive Effort: 248 kN (55590 lbf).
Weight: 106.1–110.0 t.
Train Supply: Not equipped.

37510 a	EX	EP	GROG	LR	Orion
37516 s	WC	WC	AWCA	CS	Loch Laidon
37517 as	LH	WC	AWCX	CS (S)	
37518 ar	WC	WC	AWCA	CS	
37521	G	LS	LSLO	CL	

Class 37/6. Originally refurbished for Nightstar services. Main generator replaced by alternator. UIC jumpers. Details as Class 37/5 except:
Maximum Speed: 90 mph.   **Train Brake:** Air.
Train Supply: Not equipped, but electric through wired.

37601 ad	EX	EP	GROG	LR	Perseus
37602 ar	DS	DR	XHHP	ZG (S)	
37603 a	DS	DR	XHHP	LW (S)	

37604	a	**DS**	DR	XHHP	LW (S)	
37605	ar	**DS**	DR	XHHP	ZA (S)	
37606	a	**DS**	DR	XHHP	CR (S)	
37607	ar	**DR**	HN	COTS	BH	
37608	ard	**EX**	EP	GROG	LR	Andromeda
37609	a	**DI**	DR	XHHP	LW (S)	
37610	ar	**BL**	HN	COTS	BH	
37611	ad	**EX**	EP	GROG	LR	Pegasus
37612	a	**DR**	HN	COTS	BH	

Class 37/5 continued.

37667	ars	**G**	LS	LSLO	CL	
37668	e	**WC**	WC	AWCA	CS	
37669	e	**WC**	WC	AWCA	CS	
37676	a	**WC**	WC	AWCA	CS (S)	Loch Rannoch
37685	a	**WC**	WC	AWCA	CS	Loch Arkaig
37688		**IC**	D0	MBDL	CL	Great Rocks

Class 37/7. Refurbished locomotives. Main generator replaced by alternator. Regeared (CP7) bogies. Ballast weights added. Details as Class 37/5 except:
Main Alternator: GEC G564AZ (37800) Brush BA1005A (others).
Maximum Tractive Effort: 276 kN (62000 lbf).
Weight: 120 t.   **Route Availability:** 7.

37703		**DR**	DR	XHHP	BO (S)	
37706		**WC**	WC	AWCA	CS	
37710		**LH**	WC	AWCX	CS (S)	
37712	a	**WC**	WC	AWCX	CS (S)	
37716		**DI**	DR	XHNC	KM	
37800	d	**EX**	EP	GROG	LR	Cassiopeia
37884	d	**EX**	EP	GROG	LR	Cerpheus

Class 37/9. Refurbished locomotives. New power unit. Main generator replaced by alternator. Ballast weights added. Details as Class 37/4 except:
Engine: * Mirrlees 6MB275T of 1340 kW (1800 hp) or † Ruston 6RK270T of 1340 kW (1800 hp) at 900 rpm.
Main Alternator: Brush BA15005A.
Maximum Tractive Effort: 279 kN (62680 lbf).
Weight: 120 t.   **Route Availability:** 7.
Train Supply: Not equipped.

37901	*	**EX**	EP	EPUK	LR	Mirrlees Pioneer
37905	†	**G**	UR	UKRM	LR (S)	
37906	†	**FO**	UR	UKRM	BL (S)	

Class 97/3. Class 37s refurbished for use on the Cambrian Lines which are signalled by ERTMS. Details as Class 37/0.

97301	(37100)	e	**Y**	NR	QETS	ZA	
97302	(37170)	e	**Y**	NR	QETS	ZA	Ffestiniog & Welsh Highland Railways/Rheilffyrdd Ffestiniog ac Eryri
97303	(37178)	e	**Y**	NR	QETS	ZA	
97304	(37217)	e	**Y**	NR	QETS	ZA	John Tiley

CLASS 40   ENGLISH ELECTRIC   1Co-Co1

Built: 1961 by English Electric at Vulcan Foundry, Newton-le-Willows.
Engine: English Electric 16SVT Mk2 of 1492 kW (2000 hp) at 850 rpm.
Main Generator: English Electric 822/4C.
Traction Motors: English Electric 526/5D or EE526/7D.
Maximum Tractive Effort: 231 kN (52000 lbf).
Continuous Tractive Effort: 137 kN (30900 lbf) at 18.8 mph.
Power at Rail: 1160 kW (1550 hp).   **Train Brakes:** Air & vacuum.
Brake Force: 51 t.   **Dimensions:** 21.18 x 2.78 m.
Weight: 132 t.   **Wheel Diameter:** 914/1143 mm.
Design Speed: 90 mph.   **Maximum Speed:** 90 mph.
Fuel Capacity: 3250 litres.   **Route Availability:** 6.
Train Supply: Steam heating.   **Total:** 2.

40013 Carries original number D213
40145 Carries original number 345.

| 40013 | **G** | ST | LSLO | CL | Andania |
| 40145 | **B** | 40 | CFSL | CL | |

CLASS 43   BREL/PAXMAN   Bo-Bo

Built: 1975–82 by BREL at Crewe Works.
Engine: MTU 16V4000R41R of 1680kW (2250 hp) at 1500 rpm.
(* Paxman 12VP185 of 1680 kW (2250 hp) at 1500 rpm.)
Main Alternator: Brush BA1001B.
Traction Motors: Brush TMH68–46 or GEC G417AZ (43124–152); frame mounted.
Maximum Tractive Effort: 80 kN (17980 lbf).
Continuous Tractive Effort: 46 kN (10340 lbf) at 64.5 mph.
Power at Rail: 1320 kW (1770 hp).   **Train Brakes:** Air.
Brake Force: 35 t.   **Dimensions:** 17.79 x 2.74 m.
Weight: 70.25–75.0 t.   **Wheel Diameter:** 1020 mm.
Design Speed: 125 mph.   **Maximum Speed:** 125 mph.
Fuel Capacity: 4500 litres.   **Route Availability:** 5.
Train Supply: Three-phase electric.   **Total:** 193.

† Buffer fitted.
§ Modified Great Western Railway power cars that can operate with power
door fitted short sets.

43013, 43014 & 43062 are fitted with measuring apparatus & front-end cameras.

Power cars 43013 and 43321 carry small commemorative plates to celebrate
40 years of the HST, reading "40 YEARS 1976–2016".

Non-standard liveries:

43206 and 43312 Original HST blue & yellow. Carry the numbers 43006 and
                 43112
43238 and 43274 Red

43003		**SI**	A	HAPC	HA	
43004	§	**GW**	A	EFPC	LA	Caerphilly Castle
43005	§	**GW**	A	EFPC	LA	
43009		**FB**	GW	EFPC	ZB (S)	
43010		**FB**	GW	EFPC	ZB (S)	
43012		**SI**	A	HAPC	HA	
43013	†	**Y**	P	QCAR	ZA	Mark Carne CBE
43014	†	**Y**	P	QCAR	ZA	The Railway Observer
43015		**SI**	A	HAPC	HA	
43016	§	**GW**	A	EFPC	LA	
43017		**FB**	A	SCEL	EP (S)	
43018		**FB**	A	SCEL	HA (S)	
43020		**FB**	A	EFPC	EP (S)	MTU Power. Passion. Partnership
43021		**SI**	A	HAPC	HA	
43022		**FB**	GW	EFPC	ZB (S)	
43023		**FB**	A	EFPC	EP (S)	
43024		**FB**	A	SCEL	EP (S)	
43025		**FB**	A	SCEL	EP (S)	
43026		**SI**	A	HAPC	HA	
43027		**FB**	GW	EFPC	ZB (S)	
43028		**SI**	A	HAPC	HA	
43029		**FB**	GW	EFPC	ZB (S)	
43030		**SI**	A	HAPC	ZH (S)	
43031		**SI**	A	HAPC	HA	
43032		**SI**	A	HAPC	HA	
43033		**SI**	A	HAPC	HA	
43034		**SI**	A	HAPC	HA	
43035		**SI**	A	HAPC	HA	
43036		**SI**	A	HAPC	HA	
43037		**SI**	A	HAPC	HA	
43040	§	**GW**	A	EFPC	LA	
43041	§	**GW**	A	EFPC	LA	St Catherine's Castle
43042	§	**GW**	A	EFPC	LA	Tregenna Castle
43043	*	**ST**	P	SBXL	LM (S)	
43044	*	**ST**	P	SBXL	NL (S)	
43045	*	**ST**	P	SBXL	LM (S)	
43046	*	**ST**	LS	SBXL	ZG (S)	
43047	*	**ST**	P	EMPC	NL	
43048	*	**ST**	P	EMPC	LM (S)	
43049	*	**ST**	P	EMPC	NL	Neville Hill
43050	*	**ST**	P	COTS	ZA	
43052	*	**ST**	DA	MBDL	RJ	
43053		**FB**	P	SBXL	LM (S)	
43054	*	**ST**	DA	MBDL	RJ	
43055	*	**ST**	LS	SBXL	ZG (S)	
43056		**FB**	P	SBXL	LM (S)	
43058	*	**ST**	P	EMPC	LM (S)	
43059	*	**ST**	LS	SBXL	CL (S)	
43060	*	**ST**	P	COTS	ZA	
43061	*	**ST**	P	SBXL	LM (S)	
43062		**Y**	P	QCAR	ZA	John Armitt

43063		**FB**	GW	SBXL	LA (S)	
43064	*	**ST**	P	SBXL	LM (S)	
43066	*	**ST**	DA	MBDL	RJ	
43069		**FB**	P	SBXL	LM (S)	
43070		**FB**	P	SBXL	LM (S)	
43071		**FB**	P	EFPC	LA (S)	
43073	*	**ST**	P	EMPC	NL	
43075	*	**ST**	P	SBXL	LM (S)	
43076	*	**ST**	DA	MBDL	RJ	
43078		**FB**	P	SBXL	LM (S)	
43079		**FB**	P	SBXL	LM (S)	
43081	*	**ST**	P	EMPC	LM (S)	
43082	*	**ST**	P	SBXL	LM (S)	
43083	*	**ST**	LS	SBXL	ZG (S)	
43086		**FB**	P	EFPC	LM (S)	
43087		**FB**	P	SBXL	LM (S)	
43088	§	**GW**	FG	EFPC	LA	
43089	*	**ST**	125	ICHP	RJ	
43091		**FB**	GW	SBXL	LA (S)	
43092	§	**GW**	FG	EFPC	LA	Cromwell's Castle
43093	§	**GW**	FG	EFPC	LA	Old Oak Common HST Depot 1976–2018
43094	§	**GW**	FG	EFPC	LA	St Mawes Castle
43097	§	**GW**	FG	EFPC	LA	Castle Drogo
43098	§	**GW**	FG	EFPC	LA	Walton Castle
43122	§	**GW**	FG	EFPC	LA	Dunster Castle
43124		**SI**	A	HAPC	HA	
43125		**SI**	A	HAPC	HA	
43126		**SI**	A	HAPC	HA	
43127		**SI**	A	HAPC	HA	
43128		**SI**	A	HAPC	HA	
43129		**SI**	A	HAPC	HA	
43130		**SI**	A	HAPC	HA	
43131		**SI**	A	HAPC	HA	
43132		**SI**	A	HAPC	HA	
43133		**SI**	A	HAPC	HA	
43134		**SI**	A	HAPC	HA	
43135		**SI**	A	HAPC	HA	
43136		**SI**	A	HAPC	HA	
43137		**SI**	A	HAPC	HA	
43138		**SI**	A	HAPC	HA	
43139		**SI**	A	HAPC	HA	
43140		**SI**	A	HAPC	ZH (S)	
43141		**SI**	A	HAPC	HA	
43142		**SI**	A	HAPC	HA	
43143		**SI**	A	HAPC	HA	
43144		**SI**	A	HAPC	HA	
43145		**SI**	A	HAPC	HA	
43146		**SI**	A	HAPC	HA	
43147		**SI**	A	HAPC	HA	
43148		**SI**	A	HAPC	HA	

43149	**SI**	A	HAPC	HA	
43150	**SI**	A	HAPC	HA	
43151	**SI**	A	HAPC	HA	
43152	**SI**	A	HAPC	HA	
43153 §	**GW**	FG	EFPC	LA	Chûn Castle
43154 §	**GW**	FG	EFPC	LA	Compton Castle
43155 §	**GW**	FG	EFPC	LA	Rougemont Castle
43156 §	**GW**	FG	EFPC	LA	
43158 §	**GW**	FG	EFPC	LA	Kingswear Castle
43159	**FB**	P	SBXL	LM (S)	
43160 §	**GW**	FG	EFPC	LA	
43161	**FB**	GW	SBXL	LA (S)	
43162 §	**GW**	FG	EFPC	LA	
43163	**SI**	A	HAPC	HA	
43164	**SI**	A	HAPC	HA	
43165	**FB**	A	SCEL	EP (S)	
43168	**SI**	A	HAPC	HA	
43169	**SI**	A	HAPC	HA	
43170 §	**GW**	A	EFPC	LA	Chepstow Castle
43171	**GW**	GW	EFPC	LA	
43172	**GW**	GW	EFPC	LA	
43174	**FB**	A	SCEL	EP (S)	
43175	**SI**	A	HAPC	HA	
43176	**SI**	A	HAPC	HA	
43177	**SI**	A	HAPC	HA	
43179	**SI**	A	HAPC	HA	
43180	**FB**	P	EFPC	LA (S)	
43181	**SI**	A	HAPC	HA	
43182	**SI**	A	HAPC	HA	
43183	**SI**	A	HAPC	HA	
43185	**IC**	A	SCEL	EP (S)	
43186 §	**GW**	A	EFPC	LA	Taunton Castle
43187 §	**GW**	A	EFPC	LA	
43188 §	**GW**	A	EFPC	LA	Newport Castle
43189 §	**GW**	A	EFPC	LA	Launceston Castle
43190	**FB**	A	SCEL	EP (S)	
43191	**FB**	A	EFPC	EP (S)	
43192 §	**GW**	A	EFPC	LA	Trematon Castle
43193	**FB**	P	SBXL	LM (S)	
43194 §	**GW**	FG	EFPC	LA	Okehampton Castle
43195	**FB**	FG	EFPC	LA (S)	
43196	**FB**	P	EFPC	LA (S)	
43197	**FB**	P	SBXL	LM (S)	
43198 §	**GW**	FG	EFPC	LA	Driver Stan Martin 25 June 1950 – 6 November 2004/Driver Brian Cooper 15 June 1947 – 5 October 1999

Class 43/2. Rebuilt CrossCountry and East Midlands Railway (former LNER and Grand Central) power cars. Power cars were renumbered by adding 200 to their original number or 400 to their original number (EMR), except 43123 which became 43423.

43206 (43006)	**0**	A	IECP	EP (S)	
43207 (43007)	**XC**	A	EHPC	LA	
43208 (43008)	**XC**	A	EHPC	LA	
43238 (43038)	**0**	A	EMPC	NL	
43239 (43039)	**XC**	A	EHPC	LA	
43251 (43051)	**VE**	P	EMPC	NC	
43257 (43057)	**VE**	P	EMPC	NL	
43272 (43072)	**VE**	P	EMPC	BH (S)	
43274 (43074)	**0**	P	EMPC	NL	
43277 (43077)	**VE**	P	EMPC	BH (S)	
43285 (43085)	**XC**	P	EHPC	LA	
43290 (43090)	**VE**	P	EMPC	GA (S)	
43295 (43095)	**VE**	A	EMPC	NL	
43296 (43096)	**VE**	A	EMPC	NL	
43299 (43099)	**VE**	P	EMPC	NL	
43300 (43100)	**VE**	P	IECP	NL (S)	
43301 (43101)	**XC**	P	EHPC	LA	
43302 (43102)	**VE**	P	EMPC	NL (S)	
43303 (43103)	**XC**	P	EHPC	LA	
43304 (43104)	**XC**	A	EHPC	LA	
43305 (43105)	**VE**	A	EMPC	NL	
43306 (43106)	**VE**	A	IECP	NL (S)	
43307 (43107)	**VE**	A	EMPC	NL	
43308 (43108)	**VE**	A	IECP	NL (S)	
43309 (43109)	**VE**	A	EMPC	NL	
43310 (43110)	**VE**	A	EMPC	NL	
43311 (43111)	**VE**	A	IECP	EP (S)	
43312 (43112)	**0**	A	IECP	EP (S)	
43313 (43113)	**VE**	A	IECP	LA (S)	
43314 (43114)	**VE**	A	EMPC	NL	
43315 (43115)	**VE**	A	IECP	EP (S)	
43316 (43116)	**VE**	A	EMPC	NL	
43317 (43117)	**VE**	A	EMPC	NL	
43318 (43118)	**VE**	A	EMPC	NL	
43319 (43119)	**VE**	A	EMPC	NL	
43320 (43120)	**VE**	A	EMPC	NL	
43321 (43121)	**XC**	P	EHPC	LA	
43357 (43157)	**XC**	P	EHPC	LA	
43366 (43166)	**XC**	A	EHPC	LA	
43367 (43167)	**VE**	A	IECP	EP (S)	
43378 (43178)	**XC**	A	EHPC	LA	
43384 (43184)	**XC**	A	EHPC	LA	
43423 (43123) †	**EA**	A	EMPC	DY	'VALENTA' 1972–2010
43465 (43065) †	**EA**	A	EMPC	DY	

43467 (43067) †	**EA**	A	EMPC	DY	Nottinghamshire Fire and Rescue Service/ British Transport Police Nottingham
43468 (43068) †	**EA**	A	EMPC	DY	
43480 (43080) †	**EA**	A	EMPC	DY	West Hampstead PSB
43484 (43084) †	**EA**	A	EMPC	DY	

CLASS 47   BR/BRUSH/SULZER   Co-Co

Built: 1963–67 by Brush Traction, at Loughborough or by BR at Crewe Works.
Engine: Sulzer 12LDA28C of 1920 kW (2580 hp) at 750 rpm.
Main Generator: Brush TG160-60 Mk4 or TM172-50 Mk1.
Traction Motors: Brush TM64-68 Mk1 or Mk1A.
Maximum Tractive Effort: 267 kN (60000 lbf).
Continuous Tractive Effort: 133 kN (30000 lbf) at 26 mph.
Power at Rail: 1550 kW (2080 hp).   **Train Brakes:** Air.
Brake Force: 61 t.   **Dimensions:** 19.38 x 2.79 m.
Weight: 111.5–120.6 t.   **Wheel Diameter:** 1143 mm.
Design Speed: 95 mph.   **Maximum Speed:** 95 mph.
Fuel Capacity: 3273 (+ 5887).   **Route Availability:** 6 or 7.
Train Supply: Not equipped.   **Total:** 48.

Class 47s exported for use abroad are listed in section 5 of this book.

Non-standard liveries/numbering:

47270   Also carries original number 1971.
47501   Carries original number D1944.
47614   Carries original number 1733.
47739   GBRf dark blue.
47773   Also carries original number D1755.
47798   Royal Train claret with Rail Express Systems markings.
47805   Carries original number D1935.
47810   Carries original number D1924.
47830   Also carries original number D1645.

Recent renumbering:

47593 was renumbered from 47790 in 2019.
47614 was renumbered from 47853 in 2019.

Class 47/0. Standard Design. Built with train air and vacuum brakes.

47194 +	**F**	WC	AWCX	CS (S)	
47237 x+	**WC**	WC	AWCA	CS	
47245 x+	**WC**	WC	AWCA	CS	V.E. Day 75th Anniversary
47270 +	**B**	WC	AWCA	CS	SWIFT

Class 47/3. Built with train air and vacuum brakes. Details as Class 47/0 except: **Weight:** 113.7 t.

47355 a+	**K**	WC	AWCX	CS (S)
47368	**F**	WC	AWCX	CS (S)

Class 47/4. Electric Train Supply equipment.
Details as Class 47/0 except:

Weight: 120.4–125.1 t.   **Fuel Capacity:** 3273 (+ 5537) litres.
Train Supply: Electric, index 66.   **Route Availability:** 7.

47492 x	**RX**	WC	AWCX	CS (S)
47501 x+	**GG**	LS	LSLO	CL	CRAFTSMAN
47526 x	**BL**	WC	AWCX	CS (S)
47580 x	**BL**	47	MBDL	TM	County of Essex
47593	**BL**	LS	LSLO	CL	Galloway Princess
47614 +	**B**	LS	LSLO	CL

Class 47/7. Previously fitted with an older form of TDM.
Details as Class 47/4 except:

Weight: 118.7 t.   **Fuel Capacity:** 5887 litres.
Maximum Speed: 100 mph.

47703	**FR**	HN	HNRL	ZB
47712	**IC**	CD	LSLO	CL
47714	**AR**	HN	HNRL	Old Dalby
47715	**N**	HN	HNRL	WS

Class 47/7. Former Railnet dedicated locomotives.
Details as Class 47/0 except:

Fuel Capacity: 5887 litres.

47727	**CA**	GB	GBDF	LR	Edinburgh Castle/ Caisteal Dhùn Èideann
47739	**0**	GB	GBDF	LR
47746 x	**WC**	WC	AWCA	CS	Chris Fudge 29.7.70 – 22.6.10
47749 d	**B**	GB	GBDF	LR	CITY OF TRURO
47760 x	**WC**	WC	AWCA	CS
47768	**RX**	WC	AWCX	CS (S)
47769	**V**	HN	HNRS	BH (S)	Resolve
47772 x	**WC**	WC	AWCA	CS	Carnforth TMD
47773 x	**GG**	70	MBDL	TM
47776 x	**RX**	WC	AWCX	CS (S)
47786	**WC**	WC	AWCA	CS	Roy Castle OBE
47787	**WC**	WC	AWCX	CS (S)

Class 47/4 continued. Route Availability: 6.

47798 x	**0**	NM	MBDL	YK	Prince William
47802 +	**WC**	WC	AWCA	CS
47804	**WC**	WC	AWCA	CS
47805 +	**GG**	LS	LSLO	CL	Roger Hosking MA 1925–2013
47810 +	**GG**	LS	LSLO	CL	Crewe Diesel Depot
47811 +	**GL**	LS	DHLT	CL (S)
47812 +	**RO**	RO	GROG	LR
47813 +	**RO**	RO	GROG	LR	Jack Frost
47815 +	**RO**	RO	GROG	LR	Lost Boys 68–88
47816 +	**GL**	LS	DHLT	CL (S)
47818 +	**DS**	AF	MBDL	ZG (S)

47826 +	**WC**	WC	AWCA	CS	
47828 +	**IC**	D0	AWCA	CL	
47830 +	**GG**	FL	DFLH	CB	BEECHING'S LEGACY
47832 +	**WC**	WC	AWCA	CS	
47841 +	**IC**	LS	LSLS	Margate (S)	The Institution of Mechanical Engineers
47843 +	**RB**	RO	SROG	LR (S)	
47847 +	**BL**	RO	SROG	LR (S)	
47848 +	**RB**	RO	GROG	LR	
47851 +	**WC**	WC	AWCA	CS	
47854 +	**WC**	WC	AWCA	CS	Diamond Jubilee

CLASS 50   ENGLISH ELECTRIC   Co-Co

Built: 1967–68 by English Electric at Vulcan Foundry, Newton-le-Willows.
Engine: English Electric 16CVST of 2010 kW (2700 hp) at 850 rpm.
Main Generator: English Electric 840/4B.
Traction Motors: English Electric 538/5A.
Maximum Tractive Effort: 216 kN (48500 lbf).
Continuous Tractive Effort: 147 kN (33000 lbf) at 23.5 mph.
Power at Rail: 1540 kW (2070 hp).   **Train Brakes:** Air & vacuum.
Brake Force: 59 t.   **Dimensions:** 20.88 x 2.78 m.
Weight: 116.9 t.   **Wheel Diameter:** 1092 mm.
Design Speed: 105 mph.   **Maximum Speed:** 90 mph.
Fuel Capacity: 4796 litres.   **Route Availability:** 6.
Train Supply: Electric, index 61.   **Total:** 5.

Non-standard numbering:

50007 Running with the number 50014 on one side.
50050 Also carries original number D400.

50007	**GB**	50	CFOL	KR	Hercules
50008	**B**	HH	DCRO	LR	Thunderer
50044	**B**	50	CFOL	KR	Exeter
50049	**GB**	50	CFOL	KR	Defiance
50050	**B**	NB	COFS	NM	Fearless

CLASS 52 BR/MAYBACH C-C

Built: 1961–64 by BR at Swindon Works.
Engine: Two Maybach MD655 of 1007 kW (1350 hp) each at 1500 rpm.
Transmission: Hydraulic. Voith L630rV.
Maximum Tractive Effort: 297 kN (66700 lbf).
Continuous Tractive Effort: 201 kN (45200 lbf) at 14.5 mph.
Power at Rail: 1490 kW (2000 hp).   **Train Brakes:** Air & vacuum.
Brake Force: 83 t.   **Dimensions:** 20.70 m x 2.78 m.
Weight: 110 t.   **Wheel Diameter:** 1092 mm.
Design Speed: 90 mph.   **Maximum Speed:** 90 mph.
Fuel Capacity: 3900 litres.   **Route Availability:** 6.
Train Supply: Steam heating.   **Total:** 1.

Never allocated a number in the 1972 number series.

D1015	**B**	DT	MBDL	KR	WESTERN CHAMPION

CLASS 55 ENGLISH ELECTRIC Co-Co

Built: 1961 by English Electric at Vulcan Foundry, Newton-le-Willows.
Engine: Two Napier-Deltic D18-25 of 1230 kW (1650 hp) each at 1500 rpm.
Main Generators: Two English Electric 829/1A.
Traction Motors: English Electric 538/A.
Maximum Tractive Effort: 222 kN (50000 lbf).
Continuous Tractive Effort: 136 kN (30500 lbf) at 32.5 mph.
Power at Rail: 1969 kW (2640 hp).   **Train Brakes:** Air & vacuum.
Brake Force: 51 t.   **Dimensions:** 21.18 x 2.68 m.
Weight: 100 t.   **Wheel Diameter:** 1092 mm.
Design Speed: 105 mph.   **Maximum Speed:** 100 mph.
Fuel Capacity: 3755 litres.   **Route Availability:** 5.
Train Supply: Electric, index 66.   **Total:** 4.

Non-standard numbering:

55002	Carries original number D9002.
55009	Carries original number D9009.
55016	Carries original number D9016.

55002	**GG**	NM	MBDL	YK	THE KING'S OWN YORKSHIRE LIGHT INFANTRY
55009	**B**	DP	MBDL	BH	ALYCIDON
55016	**GG**	LS	MBDL	CL (S)	GORDON HIGHLANDER
55022	**B**	LS	MBDL	CL	ROYAL SCOTS GREY

CLASS 56   BRUSH/BR/RUSTON   Co-Co

Built: 1976–84 by Electroputere at Craiova, Romania (as sub-contractors for Brush) or BREL at Doncaster or Crewe Works.
Engine: Ruston Paxman 16RK3CT of 2460 kW (3250 hp) at 900 rpm.
Main Alternator: Brush BA1101A.
Traction Motors: Brush TM73-62.
Maximum Tractive Effort: 275 kN (61800 lbf).
Continuous Tractive Effort: 240 kN (53950 lbf) at 16.8 mph.

Power at Rail: 1790 kW (2400 hp).	**Train Brakes:** Air.
Brake Force: 60 t.	**Dimensions:** 19.36 x 2.79 m.
Weight: 126 t.	**Wheel Diameter:** 1143 mm.
Design Speed: 80 mph.	**Maximum Speed:** 80 mph.
Fuel Capacity: 5228 litres.	**Route Availability:** 7.
Train Supply: Not equipped.	**Total:** 32.

All equipped with Slow Speed Control.

Class 56s exported for use abroad are listed in section 5 of this book.

Non-standard liveries:

56009 All over blue.
56303 All over dark green.

56007	**B**	GB	UKRS	LT (S)	
56009	**0**	EO	UKRS	LT (S)	
56018	**FER**	GB	UKRS	LT (S)	
56031	**FER**	GB	GBGS	LT (S)	
56032	**FER**	GB	GBGS	LT (S)	
56037	**E**	GB	GBGS	LT (S)	
56038	**FER**	GB	UKRS	LT (S)	
56049	**CS**	CS	COFS	NM	Robin of Templecombe 1938–2013
56051	**CS**	CS	COFS	NM	Survival
56060	**FER**	GB	UKRS	LT (S)	
56065	**FER**	GB	UKRS	LT (S)	
56069	**FER**	GB	GBGS	LT (S)	
56077	**LH**	GB	UKRS	LT (S)	
56078	**CS**	CS	COFS	NM	
56081	**FO**	GB	GBGD	LR	
56087	**CS**	BN	COFS	NM	
56090	**CS**	BN	COFS	NM	
56091	**DC**	DC	DCRO	LR	Driver Wayne Gaskell
					The Godfather
56094	**CS**	CS	COFS	NM	
56096	**CS**	BN	COFS	NM	
56098	**FO**	GB	GBGD	LR	
56103	**DC**	DC	DCRO	LR	
56104	**FO**	GB	UKRL	LR (S)	
56105	**CS**	BN	COFS	NM	
56106	**FER**	GB	UKRS	LR (S)	
56113	**CS**	BN	COFS	NM	
56128	**F**	GB		LT (S)	

56301 (56045)	**FA**	56	UKRL	LR	
56302 (56124)	**CS**	CS	COFS	NM	PECO The Railway Modeller
					2016 70 Years
56303 (56125)	**0**	GB	HTLX	LR	
56311 (56057)	**DC**	GB	GBGS	LT (S)	
56312 (56003)	**DC**	GB	GBGD	LR	

CLASS 57   BRUSH/GM   Co-Co

Built: 1964–65 by Brush Traction at Loughborough or BR at Crewe Works as Class 47. Rebuilt 1997–2004 by Brush Traction at Loughborough.
Engine: General Motors 12 645 E3 of 1860 kW (2500 hp) at 904 rpm.
Main Alternator: Brush BA1101D (recovered from Class 56).
Traction Motors: Brush TM64-68 Mark 1 or Mark 1A.
Maximum Tractive Effort: 244.5 kN (55000 lbf).
Continuous Tractive Effort: 140 kN (31500 lbf) at ?? mph.

Power at Rail: 1507 kW (2025 hp).	**Train Brakes:** Air.
Brake Force: 80 t.	**Dimensions:** 19.38 x 2.79 m.
Weight: 120.6 t.	**Wheel Diameter:** 1143 mm.
Design Speed: 75 mph.	**Maximum Speed:** 75 mph.
Fuel Capacity: 5550 litres.	**Route Availability:** 6
Train Supply: Not equipped.	**Total:** 33.

Non-standard livery: 57604 Original Great Western Railway green.

Class 57/0. No Train Supply Equipment. Rebuilt 1997–2000.

57001 (47356)	**WC**	WC	AWCA	CS (S)	
57002 (47322)	**DI**	DR	XHCK	KM	RAIL EXPRESS
57003 (47317)	**DI**	DR	XHCK	KM	
57004 (47347)	**DS**	DR	XHHP	LW (S)	
57005 (47350)	**AZ**	WC	AWCX	CS (S)	
57006 (47187)	**WC**	WC	AWCX	CS (S)	
57007 (47332)	**DI**	DR	XHHP	KM (S)	John Scott 12.5.45–22.5.12
57008 (47060)	**DS**	DR	XHHP	LW (S)	
57009 (47079)	**DS**	DR	XHHP	LW (S)	
57010 (47231)	**DI**	DR	XHHP	LW (S)	
57011 (47329)	**DS**	DR	XHHP	LW (S)	
57012 (47204)	**DS**	DR	XHHP	LW (S)	

Class 57/3. Electric Train Supply Equipment. Former Virgin Trains locomotives fitted with retractable Dellner couplers. Rebuilt 2002–04. Details as Class 57/0 except:

Engine: General Motors 12645F3B of 2050 kW (2750 hp) at 954 rpm.
Main Alternator: Brush BA1101F (recovered from Class 56) or Brush BA1101G.

Fuel Capacity: 5887 litres.	**Train Supply:** Electric, index 100.
Design Speed: 95 mph.	**Maximum Speed:** 95 mph.
Brake Force: 60 t.	**Weight:** 117 t.

57301 (47845) d	**DI**	P	GROG	LR	Goliath
57302 (47827) d	**DS**	DR	XHSS	ZG (S)	Chad Varah
57303 (47705) d	**DI**	P	XHSS	CR (S)	Pride of Carlisle

57304	(47807) d	**DI**	DR	XHVT	KM	Pride of Cheshire
57305	(47822) d	**VN**	P	GROG	LR	Northern Princess
57306	(47814) d	**DI**	P	XHAC	KM	Her Majesty's Railway Inspectorate 175
57307	(47225) d	**DI**	DR	XHVT	KM	LADY PENELOPE
57308	(47846) d	**DI**	DR	XHVT	KM	Jamie Ferguson
57309	(47806) d	**DI**	DR	XHVT	KM	Pride of Crewe
57310	(47831) d	**DR**	P	GROG	LR	Pride of Cumbria
57311	(47817) d	**DS**	DR	XHSS	BO (S)	Thunderbird
57312	(47330) d	**RO**	P	GROG	LR	
57313	(47371)	**PC**	WC	AWCA	CS	Scarborough Castle
57314	(47372)	**WC**	WC	AWCA	CS	
57315	(47234)	**WC**	WC	AWCA	CS	
57316	(47290)	**WC**	WC	AWCA	CS	

Class 57/6. Electric Train Supply Equipment. Prototype ETS loco. Rebuilt 2001. Details as Class 57/0 except:

Main Alternator: Brush BA1101E.   **Fuel Capacity:** 3273 litres.
Train Supply: Electric, index 95.   **Weight:** 113t.
Design Speed: 95 mph.   **Maximum Speed:** 95 mph.
Brake Force: 60 t.

| 57601 | (47825) | **PC** | WC | AWCA | CS | Windsor Castle |

Class 57/6. Electric Train Supply Equipment. Great Western Railway locomotives. Rebuilt 2004. Details as Class 57/3.

57602	(47337)	**GW**	P	EFOO	PZ	Restormel Castle
57603	(47349)	**GW**	P	EFOO	PZ	Tintagel Castle
57604	(47209)	**O**	P	EFOO	PZ	PENDENNIS CASTLE
57605	(47206)	**GW**	P	EFOO	PZ	Totnes Castle

CLASS 58   BREL/RUSTON   Co-Co

Built: 1983–87 by BREL at Doncaster Works.
Engine: Ruston Paxman 12RK3ACT of 2460 kW (3300 hp) at 1000 rpm.
Main Alternator: Brush BA1101B.
Traction Motors: Brush TM73-62.
Maximum Tractive Effort: 275 kN (61800 lbf).
Continuous Tractive Effort: 240 kN (53950 lbf) at 17.4 mph.
Power at Rail: 1780 kW (2387 hp).   **Train Brakes:** Air.
Brake Force: 60 t.   **Dimensions:** 19.13 x 2.72 m.
Weight: 130 t.   **Wheel Diameter:** 1120 mm.
Design Speed: 80 mph.   **Maximum Speed:** 80 mph.
Fuel Capacity: 4214 litres.   **Route Availability:** 7.
Train Supply: Not equipped.   **Total:** 2.

All equipped with Slow Speed Control.

Class 58s exported for use abroad are listed in section 5 of this book.

| 58012 | **F** | PO | BL (S) |
| 58023 | **ML** | PO | LR (S) |

CLASS 59   GENERAL MOTORS   Co-Co

Built: 1985 (59001–004) or 1989 (59005) by General Motors, La Grange, Illinois, USA or 1990 (59101–104), 1994 (59201) and 1995 (59202–206) by General Motors, London, Ontario, Canada.
Engine: General Motors 16-645E3C two stroke of 2460 kW (3300 hp) at 904 rpm.
Main Alternator: General Motors AR11 MLD-D14A.
Traction Motors: General Motors D77B.
Maximum Tractive Effort: 506 kN (113550 lbf).
Continuous Tractive Effort: 291 kN (65300 lbf) at 14.3 mph.

Power at Rail: 1889 kW (2533 hp).	**Train Brakes:** Air.
Brake Force: 69 t.	**Dimensions:** 21.35 x 2.65 m.
Weight: 121 t.	**Wheel Diameter:** 1067 mm.
Design Speed: 60 (* 75) mph.	**Maximum Speed:** 60 (* 75) mph.
Fuel Capacity: 4546 litres.	**Route Availability:** 7.
Train Supply: Not equipped.	**Total:** 15.

Class 59/0. Owned by Freightliner and GB Railfreight.

59001	**AI**	FL	DFHG	MD	YEOMAN ENDEAVOUR
59002	**AI**	FL	DFHG	MD	ALAN J DAY
59003	**GB**	GB	GBYH	RR	YEOMAN HIGHLANDER
59004	**AI**	FL	DFHG	MD	PAUL A HAMMOND
59005	**AI**	FL	DFHG	MD	KENNETH J PAINTER

Class 59/1. Owned by Freightliner,

59101	**HA**	FL	DFHG	MD	Village of Whatley
59102	**HA**	FL	DFHG	MD	Village of Chantry
59103	**HA**	FL	DFHG	MD	Village of Mells
59104	**HA**	FL	DFHG	MD	Village of Great Elm

Class 59/2. Owned by DB Cargo.

59201	*	**DB**	FL	DFHG	MD	
59202	*	**DB**	FL	DFHG	MD	Alan Meddows Taylor MD Mendip Rail Limited
59203	*	**FG**	FL	DFHG	MD	
59204	*	**DB**	FL	DFHG	MD	
59205	*b	**DB**	FL	DFHG	MD	
59206	*b	**FG**	FL	DFHG	MD	John F. Yeoman Rail Pioneer

CLASS 60   BRUSH/MIRRLEES   Co-Co

Built: 1989–93 by Brush Traction at Loughborough.
Engine: Mirrlees 8MB275T of 2310 kW (3100 hp) at 1000 rpm.
Main Alternator: Brush BA1006A.
Traction Motors: Brush TM2161A.
Maximum Tractive Effort: 500 kN (106500 lbf).
Continuous Tractive Effort: 336 kN (71570 lbf) at 17.4 mph.
Power at Rail: 1800 kW (2415 hp).   **Train Brakes:** Air.
Brake Force: 74 t (+ 62 t).   **Dimensions:** 21.34 x 2.64 m.
Weight: 129 t (+ 131 t).   **Wheel Diameter:** 1118 mm.
Design Speed: 62 mph.   **Maximum Speed:** 60 mph.
Fuel Capacity: 4546 (+ 5225) litres.   **Route Availability:** 8.
Train Supply: Not equipped.   **Total:** 100.

All equipped with Slow Speed Control.

* Refurbished locomotives.

60034, 60064, 60070, 60072, 60073, 60077, 60084 and 60090 carry their names on one side only.

60500 originally carried the number 60016.

Non-standard and Advertising liveries:

60026   Beacon Rail (blue).
60028   Cappagh (blue).
60066   Powering Drax (silver).
60074   Puma Energy (grey).
60081   Original Great Western Railway green.
60099   Tata Steel (silver).

60001	*	**DB**	DB	WCAT	TO
60002	+*	**CS**	BN	GBTG	TO
60003	+	**E**	DB	WQCA	TO (S) FREIGHT TRANSPORT ASSOCIATION
60004	+	**E**	GB	WQCA	TO (S)
60005	+	**E**	DB	WQDA	TO (S)
60007	+*	**DB**	DB	WCBT	TO The Spirit of Tom Kendell
60008		**E**	GB	WQCA	TO (S) Sir William McAlpine
60009	+	**E**	GB	WQCA	TO (S)
60010	+*	**DB**	DB	WCBT	TO
60011		**DB**	DB	WCAT	TO
60012	+	**E**	DB	WQCA	TO (S)
60013		**EG**	DB	WQCA	TO (S) Robert Boyle
60014		**EG**	GB	WQCA	TO (S)
60015	+*	**DB**	DB	WCBT	TO
60017	+*	**DB**	DB	WCBT	TO
60018		**E**	GB	WQCA	TO (S)
60019	*	**DB**	DB	WCAT	TO Port of Grimsby & Immingham
60020	+*	**DB**	DB	WCBT	TO The Willows
60021	+*	**GB**	BN	GBTG	TO PENYGHENT
60022	+	**E**	DB	WQCA	TO (S)
60023	+	**E**	DB	WQCA	TO (S)

60024	*	**DB**	DB	WCAT	TO		Clitheroe Castle
60025	+	**E**	DB	WQCA	TO (S)		
60026	+*	**O**	BN	GBTG	TO		HELVELLYN
60027	+	**E**	DB	WQCA	TO (S)		
60028	+	**O**	DC	DCRS	TO		
60029		**DC**	DC	DCRS	TO		Ben Nevis
60030	+	**E**	DB	WQCA	TO (S)		
60031		**E**	DB	WQCA	TO (S)		
60032		**F**	DB	WQCA	TO (S)		
60033	+	**CU**	DB	WQCA	TO (S)		Tees Steel Express
60034		**EG**	DB	WQCA	TO (S)		Carnedd Llewelyn
60035		**E**	DB	WQBA	TO (S)		
60036		**E**	DB	WQCA	TO (S)		GEFCO
60037	+	**E**	DB	WQCA	TO (S)		
60038	+	**E**	DB	WQCA	TO (S)		
60039	*	**DB**	DB	WCAT	TO		Dove Holes
60040	*	**DB**	DB	WCAT	TO		The Territorial Army Centenary
60041	+	**E**	DB	WQCA	TO (S)		
60042		**E**	DB	WQCA	TO (S)		
60043		**E**	DB	WQCA	TO (S)		
60044	*	**DB**	DB	WCAT	TO		Dowlow
60045		**E**	DB	WQBA	TO (S)		The Permanent Way Institution
60046	+	**DC**	DC	DCRC	TO		William Wilberforce
60047	*	**CS**	BN	GBTG	TO		
60048		**E**	DB	WQCA	TO (S)		
60049		**E**	DB	WQBA	TO (S)		
60051	+	**E**	DB	WQCA	TO (S)		
60052	+	**E**	DB	WQCA	TO (S)		Glofa Twr – The last deep mine in Wales – Tower Colliery
60053		**E**	DB	WQCA	TO (S)		
60054	+*	**DB**	DB	WCBT	TO		
60055	+	**DC**	DC	DCRS	TO		Thomas Barnardo
60056	+*	**CS**	BN	GBTG	TO		
60057		**EG**	DB	WQCA	TO (S)		Adam Smith
60058	+	**E**	DB	WQCA	TO (S)		
60059	+*	**DB**	DB	WCBT	TO		Swinden Dalesman
60060		**EG**	PO	WQDA	TO (S)		
60061		**F**	DB	WQCA	TO (S)		
60062	*	**DB**	DB	WCAT	TO		Stainless Pioneer
60063	*	**DB**	DB	WCAT	TO		
60064	+	**EG**	DB	WQCA	TO (S)		Back Tor
60065		**E**	DB	WCAT	TO		Spirit of JAGUAR
60066	*	**AL**	DB	WCAT	TO		
60067		**EG**	DB	WQCA	TO (S)		
60068		**EG**	DB	WQCA	TO (S)		
60069		**E**	DB	WQCA	TO (S)		Slioch
60070	+	**F**	DB	WQCA	TO (S)		John Loudon McAdam
60071	+	**E**	DB	WQBA	TO (S)		Ribblehead Viaduct
60072		**EG**	DB	WQCA	TO (S)		Cairn Toul
60073		**EG**	DB	WQCA	TO (S)		Cairn Gorm
60074	*	**AL**	DB	WCAT	TO		Luke

▲ 08598 and 08600 are seen at AV Dawson's rail terminal in Middlesbrough on 25/07/20.　**Andrew Mason**

▼ HNRC-liveried 09106 / "6" shunts at the Celsa Steel UK terminal in Cardiff on 25/06/20.　**Martin Turner**

▲ In white livery and carrying internal No. "3", 20906 is seen at Earles Sidings having hauled a train from Hope Cement Works on 22/08/20.   **Ian Beardsley**

▼ BR blue-liveried 31128 passes Barrow-on-Trent with 5Z34 12.50 Barrow Hill–Lichfield TV Sidings empty stock on 18/11/19.   **John Coleman**

▲ West Coast Railway Company maroon-liveried 33029 leads a London Paddington–Lancaster Branch Line Society railtour at Coventry on 09/03/20.
Brad Joyce

▼ Europhoenix-liveried 37608 "Andromeda" passes Hodthorpe, near Whitwell, with a 11.01 Worksop Down Yard–Old Dalby hauling Elizabeth Line EMU 345 045 on 18/05/20.
Ian Beardsley

▲ BR Blue-liveried 40145 passes Blea Moor, near Ribblehead, with the 14.38 Appleby–Skipton Rail Charter Services train on 12/09/20.   **Dave Gommersall**

▼ Great Western Railway-liveried "Castle Class" four-coach HST 43016+43160 passes Bethany, near Saltash, with the 13.11 Penzance–Plymouth on 13/09/20.
Tony Christie

▲ CrossCountry HST 43301+43357 is seen at Woodhouse with the diverted 09.27 Plymouth–Glasgow Central on 12/07/20.　　**Ian Beardsley**

▼ BR two-tone green-liveried 47805 passes Besford, Worcestershire with 5Z47 11.31 Long Marston–Eastleigh Works stock movement on 12/03/20.
Dave Gommersall

▲ BR blue-liveried 50008 is seen at Besford hauling 20132, 20118 and 56091 from Leicester to Bristol Barton Hill on 03/12/19.　　　**Dave Gommersall**

▼ Devon & Cornwall Railways-liveried 56103 passes Loughborough with 4Z20 17.58 Leicester Humberstone Road–Chaddesden Sidings box wagons on 13/06/20.　　　**Paul Biggs**

▲ Pullman-liveried 57313 and 57601 pass Stafford with a 5M43 Southall–Carnforth stock movement on 16/03/20 **Brad Joyce**

▼ New Freightliner-liveried 59206 passes Hungerford Common with 7C64 15.25 Acton–Merehead stone empties on 17/09/20. **Tony Bartlett**

▲ GBRf-liveried 60021 is seen at Marcheys House Junction on the Blyth & Tyne line with 6N85 08.41 Lynemouth Power Station–Tyne Dock biomass empties on 04/09/20. **Jamie Squibbs**

▼ Cappagh-liveried and DC Rail-operated 60028 passes Saxilby with 6Z63 15.00 Rossington–Chaddesden Sidings (Derby) empty box wagons on 08/08/20. **Robert Pritchard**

▲ DB Cargo-liveried 66115 is seen near Saxilby with 4E25 11.29 Bow–Heck empty concrete bricks on 15/06/20.
Robert Pritchard

▲ GBRf-liveried 66769 is seen near Saxilby with 4Z81 11.34 Rotherham Masborough–Felixstowe intermodal on 16/04/20.　**Robert Pritchard**

▼ Colas Rail-liveried 67027 and 67023 top-and-tail a Tyseley–Weymouth Network Rail test train at Wyke Champflower, near Bruton, on 12/08/20.　**Glen Batten**

▲ TransPennine Express-liveried 68032 "Destroyer" leaves Seamer hauling a set of Mark 5A coaches on the 09.57 Scarborough–York on 08/08/20 (terminating at York due to engineering works). **Andrew Mason**

▲ Colas Rail-liveried 70805 passes Saxilby with 6E98 20.45 Aberdeen–Spalding china clay slurry on 02/06/20. **Robert Pritchard**

▼ Network Rail yellow-liveried 73952 is seen on display at the Locomotive Services Crewe open day on 08/06/19. **Robert Pritchard**

▲ Freightliner-liveried 86639+86609 pass Grendon, Northamptonshire with 4L97 06.15 Trafford Park–Felixstowe intermodal on 07/08/20. **Andrew Mason**

▲ New DRS-liveried 88005 passes Carluke with 4S44 12.16 Daventry–Mossend intermodal on 20/05/20.   **Robin Ralston**

▼ InterCity-liveried 90002 leads DVT 82139 and a set of Mark 3 coaches through Winwick with 5Z92 12.33 Preston–Crewe test run on 21/09/20.   **Alan Hart**

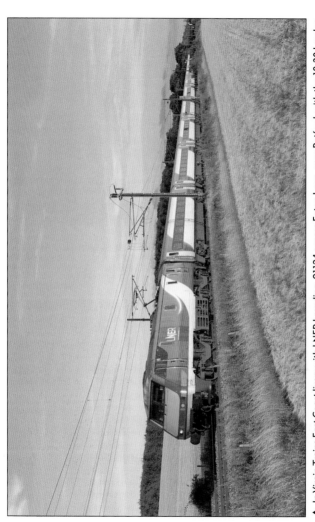

▲ In Virgin Trains East Coast livery with LNER branding, 91124 passes Eaton Lane, near Retford, with the 18.30 London King's Cross–Edinburgh on 06/08/20.

Ian Beardsley

▲ GBRf-liveried 92043 passes Leggatfoot, south of Carstairs, with the previous evening's 23.50 London Euston–Glasgow Central/Edinburgh Lowland Sleeper on 28/06/19. **Robin Ralston**

▼ Eurotunnel Class 9/8 9809 leaves the Cheriton terminal before entering the Channel Tunnel with a car shuttle on 05/08/18. **Robert Pritchard**

60075	E	DB	WQCA	TO (S)	
60076 *	CS	BN	GBTG	TO	Dunbar
60077 +	EG	DB	WQCA	TO (S)	Canisp
60078	ML	DB	WQCA	TO (S)	
60079 *	DB	DB	WQBA	TO (S)	
60080 +	E	DB	WQCA	TO (S)	
60081 +	O	LS	WQDA	TO (S)	
60082	EG	DB	WQCA	CE (S)	
60083	E	DB	WQCA	TO (S)	
60084	EG	DB	WQCA	TO (S)	Cross Fell
60085 *	CS	BN	GBTG	TO	
60087 *	CS	BN	GBTG	TO	
60088	F	DB	WQCA	TO (S)	
60089 +	E	DB	WQCA	TO (S)	
60090 +	EG	DB	WQCA	TO (S)	Quinag
60091 +*	DB	DB	WCBT	TO	Barry Needham
60092 +*	DB	DB	WCBT	TO	
60093	E	DB	WQCA	TO (S)	
60094	E	DB	WQCA	TO (S)	Rugby Flyer
60095 *	GB	BN	GBTG	TO	
60096 +*	CS	BN	GBTG	TO	
60097 +	E	DB	WQCA	TO (S)	
60098 +	E	DB	WQCA	TO (S)	
60099	AL	DB	WQCA	TO	
60100 *	DB	DB	WCAT	TO	Midland Railway - Butterley
60500	E	DB	WQCA	TO (S)	

CLASS 66   GENERAL MOTORS/EMD   Co-Co

Built: 1998–2008 by General Motors/EMD, London, Ontario, Canada (Model JT42CWR (low emission locomotives Model JT42CWRM)) or 2013–16 by EMD/Progress Rail, Muncie, Indiana (66752–779).
Engine: General Motors 12N-710G3B-EC two stroke of 2385 kW (3200 hp) at 904 rpm. 66752–779 GM 12N-710G3B-T2.
Main Alternator: General Motors AR8/CA6.
Traction Motors: General Motors D43TR.
Maximum Tractive Effort: 409 kN (92000 lbf).
Continuous Tractive Effort: 260 kN (58390 lbf) at 15.9 mph.

Power at Rail: 1850 kW (2480 hp).	**Train Brakes:** Air.
Brake Force: 68 t.	**Dimensions:** 21.35 x 2.64 m.
Weight: 127 t.	**Wheel Diameter:** 1120 mm.
Design Speed: 87.5 mph.	**Maximum Speed:** 75 mph.
Fuel Capacity: 6550 litres.	**Route Availability:** 7.
Train Supply: Not equipped.	**Total:** 388.

All equipped with Slow Speed Control.

Class 66s previously used in the UK but now in use abroad are listed in section 5 of this book. Some of the DBC 66s moved to France return to Great Britain from time to time for maintenance or operational requirements.

Class 66 delivery dates. The Class 66 design and delivery evolved over an 18-year period, with more than 400 locomotives delivered. For clarity the delivery dates (by year) for each batch of locomotives is as follows:

66001–250	EWS (now DB Cargo). 1998–2000 (some now in use in France or Poland, ten sold to GB Railfreight and five on long-term hire to DRS).
66301–305	Fastline. 2008. Now used by DRS.
66401–410	DRS. 2003. Now in use with GB Railfreight or Colas Rail and renumbered 66733–737 and 66742–746 (66734 since scrapped).
66411–420	DRS. 2006. Now leased by Freightliner (66411/412/417 exported to Poland).
66421–430	DRS. 2007
66431–434	DRS. 2008
66501–505	Freightliner. 1999
66506–520	Freightliner. 2000
66521–525	Freightliner. 2000 (66521 since scrapped).
66526–531	Freightliner. 2001
66532–537	Freightliner. 2001
66538–543	Freightliner. 2001
66544–553	Freightliner. 2001
66554	Freightliner. 2002†
66555–566	Freightliner. 2002
66567–574	Freightliner. 2003. 66573–574 now used by Colas Rail and renumbered 66846–847.
66575–577	Freightliner. 2004. Now used by Colas Rail and renumbered 66848–850.
66578–581	Freightliner. 2005. Now used by GBRf and renumbered 66738–741.
66582–594	Freightliner. 2007 (66582/583/584/586 exported to Poland).
66595–599	Freightliner. 2008 (66595 exported to Poland).
66601–606	Freightliner. 2000
66607–612	Freightliner. 2002 (66607/609/611/612 exported to Poland)
66613–618	Freightliner. 2003
66619–622	Freightliner. 2005
66623–625	Freightliner. 2007 (66624/625 exported to Poland).
66701–707	GB Railfreight. 2001
66708–712	GB Railfreight. 2002
66713–717	GB Railfreight. 2003
66718–722	GB Railfreight. 2006
66723–727	GB Railfreight. 2006
66728–732	GB Railfreight. 2008
66747–749	Built in 2008 as 20078968-004/006/007 (DE 6313/15/16) for Crossrail AG in the Netherlands but never used. Sold to GB Railfreight in 2012.
66750–751	Built in 2003 as 20038513-01/04 and have worked in the Netherlands, Germany and Poland. GBRf secured these two locomotives on lease in 2013.
66752–772	GB Railfreight. 2014
66773–779	GB Railfreight. 2016
66780–789	GB Railfreight. 1998–2000. Former DBC locomotives acquired in 2017 that have been renumbered in the GBRf number series.

66790–792	Built in 2002 as 20018352-3/4/5 (T66403–405) for CargoNet, Norway. Sold to Beacon Rail and leased to GBRf from 2019.
66793–797	Second-hand locos being imported from Germany. 66793/794 ex-HHPI 29004/005 built 2003. Full details of others awaited.
66951–952	Freightliner. 2004
66953–957	Freightliner. 2008 (66954 exported to Poland).

Advertising and non-standard liveries:

66109	PD Ports (dark blue).
66587	Ocean Network Express (pink with white stripes).
66709	MSC – blue with images of a container ship.
66718	London Underground 150, (black).
66720	Day and night (various colours, different on each side).
66721	London Underground 150 (white with tube map images). Also carries the numbers 1933 and 2013.
66723	Also carries the number ZA723.
66731	Thank you NHS (blue with orange cabsides).
66747	Newell & Wright (blue, white & red).
66775	Also carries the number F231.
66779	BR dark green.
66780	Cemex (grey, blue & red).
66783	Biffa (red & orange).
66791, 66793, 66794	Beacon Rail (blue).

Class 66/0. DB Cargo-operated locomotives.

All fitted with Swinghead Automatic "Buckeye" Combination Couplers except 66001 and 66002.

66031, 66091, 66108, 66122 and 66126 are on long-term hire to DRS.

† Fitted with additional lights and drawgear for Lickey banking duties.

t Fitted with tripcocks for working over London Underground tracks between Harrow-on-the-Hill and Amersham.

66001 t	**DB**	DB	WBAE	TO	
66002	**E**	DB	WBAE	TO	
66003	**E**	DB	WBAE	TO	
66004	**E**	DB	WBAR	TO	
66005	**MT**	DB	WBAE	TO	Maritime Intermodal One
66006	**E**	DB	WBAR	TO	
66007	**E**	DB	WBAR	TO	
66009	**DB**	DB	WBAE	TO	
66011	**E**	DB	WBAE	TO	
66012	**E**	DB	WBAE	TO	
66013	**E**	DB	WBAE	TO	
66014	**E**	DB	WBAR	TO	
66015	**E**	DB	WBAR	TO	
66017 t	**DB**	DB	WBAR	TO	
66018	**DB**	DB	WBAE	TO	
66019 t	**DB**	DB	WBAR	TO	
66020	**DB**	DB	WBAE	TO	
66021	**DB**	DB	WBAR	TO	

66023	E	DB	WBAT	TO	
66024	E	DB	WBAE	TO	
66025	E	DB	WBAR	TO	
66027	DB	DB	WBAE	TO	
66030	E	DB	WBRT	TO	
66031	E	DB	XHIM	KM	
66034	DB	DB	WBAE	TO	
66035	DB	DB	WBAE	TO	Resourceful
66037	E	DB	WBAR	TO	
66039	E	DB	WBAE	TO	
66040	E	DB	WBAR	TO	
66041	DB	DB	WBAR	TO	
66043	E	DB	WQBA	TO (S)	
66044	DB	DB	WBAE	TO	
66047	MT	DB	WBAE	TO	Maritime Intermodal Two
66050	E	DB	WBAE	TO	EWS Energy
66051	MT	DB	WBAR	TO	Maritime Intermodal Four
66053	E	DB	WBAE	TO	
66054	E	DB	WBAR	TO	
66055 †	DB	DB	WBLT	TO	Alain Thauvette
66056 †	E	DB	WBLE	TO	
66057 †	E	DB	WBLE	TO	
66059 †	E	DB	WBLE	TO	
66060	E	DB	WBRT	TO	
66061	E	DB	WBAE	TO	
66063	E	DB	WBAE	TO	
66065	DB	DB	WBAR	TO	
66066	DB	DB	WBAR	TO	Geoff Spencer
66067	E	DB	WBAR	TO	
66068	E	DB	WBAR	TO	
66069	E	DB	WBAR	TO	
66070	DB	DB	WBAE	TO	
66074	DB	DB	WBAE	TO	
66075	E	DB	WBAE	TO	
66076	E	DB	WBAE	TO	
66077	DB	DB	WBAR	TO	Benjamin Gimbert G.C.
66078	DB	DB	WBAE	TO	
66079	E	DB	WBAR	TO	James Nightall G.C.
66080	E	DB	WBAE	TO	
66082	DB	DB	WBAE	TO	
66083	E	DB	WBAR	TO	
66084	E	DB	WBAR	TO	
66085	DB	DB	WBAR	TO	
66086	E	DB	WBAE	TO	
66087	E	DB	WBAE	TO	
66088	E	DB	WBAE	TO	
66089	E	DB	WBAR	TO	
66090	MT	DB	WBAE	TO	Maritime Intermodal Six
66091	DR	DB	XHIM	KM	
66092	E	DB	WBAE	TO	
66093	E	DB	WBAE	TO	

66094	**DB**	DB	WBAE	TO	
66095	**E**	DB	WBAE	TO	
66096	**E**	DB	WBAE	TO	
66097	**DB**	DB	WBAE	TO	
66098	**E**	DB	WBAE	TO	
66099 r	**E**	DB	WBRT	TO	
66100 r	**DB**	DB	WBBE	TO	Armistice 100 1918–2018
66101 r	**DB**	DB	WBBE	TO	
66102 r	**E**	DB	WBBE	TO	
66103 r	**E**	DB	WBBE	TO	
66104 r	**DB**	DB	WBBT	TO	
66105 r	**DB**	DB	WBAR	TO	
66106 r	**E**	DB	WBBE	TO	
66107 r	**DB**	DB	WBBT	TO	
66108 r	**E**	DB	XHIM	KM	
66109	**AL**	DB	WBAR	TO	Teesport Express
66110 r	**E**	DB	WBBE	TO	
66111 r	**E**	DB	WBRT	TO	
66112 r	**E**	DB	WBBE	TO	
66113 r	**DB**	DB	WBBE	TO	
66114 r	**DB**	DB	WBRT	TO	
66115	**DB**	DB	WBAE	TO	
66116	**E**	DB	WBRT	TO	
66117	**DB**	DB	WBAE	TO	
66118	**DB**	DB	WBAE	TO	
66119	**E**	DB	WBAE	TO	
66120	**E**	DB	WBAE	TO	
66121	**E**	DB	WBAE	TO	
66122	**E**	DB	XHIM	KM	
66124	**DB**	DB	WBAR	TO	
66125	**E**	DB	WBAE	TO	
66126	**E**	DB	XHIM	KM	
66127	**E**	DB	WBAT	TO	
66128	**DB**	DB	WBAE	TO	
66129	**E**	DB	WBAR	TO	
66130	**DB**	DB	WBAR	TO	
66131	**DB**	DB	WBAE	TO	
66133	**E**	DB	WBAE	TO	
66134	**DB**	DB	WBAE	TO	
66135	**DB**	DB	WBAE	TO	
66136	**DB**	DB	WBAE	TO	
66137	**DB**	DB	WBAE	TO	
66138	**E**	DB	WQBA	TO (S)	
66139	**E**	DB	WBAE	TO	
66140	**E**	DB	WBAE	TO	
66142	**MT**	DB	WBAR	TO	Maritime Intermodal Three
66143	**E**	DB	WBRT	TO	
66144	**E**	DB	WBAR	TO	
66145	**E**	DB	WQBA	TO (S)	
66147	**E**	DB	WBAE	TO	
66148	**MT**	DB	WBAE	TO	Maritime Intermodal Seven

66149	**DB**	DB	WBAE	TO	
66150	**DB**	DB	WBAE	TO	
66151	**E**	DB	WBRT	TO	
66152	**DB**	DB	WBAE	TO	Derek Holmes Railway Operator
66154	**E**	DB	WBAE	TO	
66155	**E**	DB	WBRT	TO	
66156	**E**	DB	WBAE	TO	
66158	**E**	DB	WBAE	TO	
66160	**E**	DB	WBAR	TO	
66161	**E**	DB	WBRT	TO	
66162	**MT**	DB	WBAR	TO	Maritime Intermodal Five
66164	**E**	DB	WBAE	TO	
66165	**DB**	DB	WBAR	TO	
66167	**DB**	DB	WBAE	TO	
66168	**E**	DB	WBAR	TO	
66169	**E**	DB	WBAR	TO	
66170	**E**	DB	WBAE	TO	
66171	**E**	DB	WBAR	TO	
66172	**E**	DB	WBAE	TO	PAUL MELLENEY
66174	**E**	DB	WBRT	TO	
66175	**DB**	DB	WBAE	TO	Rail Riders Express
66176	**E**	DB	WBAR	TO	
66177	**E**	DB	WBAT	TO	
66181	**E**	DB	WBAR	TO	
66182	**DB**	DB	WQAB	TO (S)	
66183	**E**	DB	WBRT	TO	
66185	**DB**	DB	WBAE	TO	DP WORLD London Gateway
66186	**E**	DB	WBRT	TO	
66187	**E**	DB	WBAE	TO	
66188	**E**	DB	WBAR	TO	
66192	**DB**	DB	WBAR	TO	
66194	**E**	DB	WBRT	TO	
66197	**E**	DB	WBAE	TO	
66198	**E**	DB	WBAR	TO	
66199	**E**	DB	WBRT	TO	
66200	**E**	DB	WBAE	TO	
66206	**DB**	DB	WBAR	TO	
66207	**E**	DB	WBAE	TO	
66221	**E**	DB	WBAR	TO	
66230	**DB**	DB	WQBA	TO (S)	

Class 66/3. Former Fastline-operated locomotives now operated by DRS. Low emission. Details as Class 66/0 except:

Engine: EMD 12N-710G3B-T2 two stroke of 2420 kW (3245 hp) at 904 rpm.
Traction Motors: General Motors D43TRC.
Fuel Capacity: 5150 litres.

66301	**DR**	BN	XHIM	KM	Kingmoor TMD
66302	**DR**	BN	XHIM	KM	Endeavour
66303	**DR**	BN	XHIM	KM	
66304	**DR**	BN	XHIM	KM	
66305	**DR**	BN	XHIM	KM	

Class 66/4. Low emission. Macquarie Group-owned. Details as Class 66/3.

66413	**FG**	AK	DFIN	LD	Lest We Forget
66414	**FH**	AK	DFIN	LD	
66415	**FG**	AK	DFIN	LD	You Are Never Alone
66416	**FH**	AK	DFIN	LD	
66418	**FH**	AK	DFIN	LD	PATRIOT – IN MEMORY OF FALLEN RAILWAY EMPLOYEES
66419	**FG**	AK	DFIN	LD	
66420	**FH**	AK	DFIN	LD	
66421	**DR**	AK	XHIM	KM	Gresty Bridge TMD
66422	**DR**	AK	XHIM	KM	
66423	**DR**	AK	XHIM	KM	
66424	**DR**	AK	XHIM	KM	
66425	**DR**	AK	XHIM	KM	
66426	**DR**	AK	XHIM	KM	
66427	**DR**	AK	XHIM	KM	
66428	**DR**	AK	XHIM	KM	Carlisle Eden Mind
66429	**DR**	AK	XHIM	KM	
66430	**DR**	AK	XHIM	KM	
66431	**DR**	AK	XHIM	KM	
66432	**DR**	AK	XHIM	KM	
66433	**DR**	AK	XHIM	KM	
66434	**DR**	AK	XHIM	KM	

Class 66/5. Standard design. Freightliner-operated locomotives. Details as Class 66/0.

66501	**FL**	P	DFIM	LD	Japan 2001
66502	**FG**	P	DFIM	LD	Basford Hall Centenary 2001
66503	**FL**	P	DFIM	LD	The RAILWAY MAGAZINE
66504	**FH**	P	DFIM	LD	
66505	**FL**	P	DFIM	LD	
66506	**FL**	E	DFIM	LD	Crewe Regeneration
66507	**FL**	E	DFIM	LD	
66508	**FL**	E	DFIM	LD	
66509	**FL**	E	DFIM	LD	
66510	**FL**	E	DFIM	LD	
66511	**FL**	E	DFIM	LD	
66512	**FL**	E	DFIM	LD	
66513	**FL**	E	DFIM	LD	
66514	**FL**	E	DFIM	LD	
66515	**FL**	E	DFIM	LD	
66516	**FL**	E	DFIM	LD	
66517	**FL**	E	DFIM	LD	
66518	**FL**	E	DFIM	LD	
66519	**FL**	E	DFIM	LD	
66520	**FL**	E	DFIM	LD	
66522	**FL**	E	DFIM	LD	
66523	**FL**	E	DFIM	LD	
66524	**FL**	E	DFIM	LD	
66525	**FL**	E	DFIM	LD	
66526	**FL**	P	DFIM	LD	Driver Steve Dunn (George)

66528	**FH**	P	DFIM	LD	Madge Elliot MBE
					Borders Railway Opening 2015
66529	**FL**	P	DFIM	LD	
66531	**FL**	P	DFIM	LD	
66532	**FL**	P	DFIM	LD	P&O Nedlloyd Atlas
66533	**FL**	P	DFIM	LD	Hanjin Express/Senator Express
66534	**FL**	P	DFIM	LD	OOCL Express
66536	**FL**	P	DFIM	LD	
66537	**FL**	P	DFIM	LD	
66538	**FL**	E	DFIM	LD	
66539	**FL**	E	DFIM	LD	
66540	**FL**	E	DFIM	LD	Ruby
66541	**FL**	E	DFIM	LD	
66542	**FL**	E	DFIM	LD	
66543	**FL**	E	DFIM	LD	
66544	**FL**	P	DFIM	LD	
66545	**FL**	P	DFIM	LD	
66546	**FL**	P	DFIM	LD	
66547	**FL**	P	DFIM	LD	
66548	**FL**	P	DFIM	LD	
66549	**FL**	P	DFIM	LD	
66550	**FL**	P	DFIM	LD	
66551	**FL**	P	DFIM	LD	
66552	**FL**	P	DFIM	LD	Maltby Raider
66553	**FL**	P	DFIM	LD	
66554	**FL**	E	DFIM	LD	
66555	**FL**	E	DFIM	LD	
66556	**FL**	E	DFIM	LD	
66557	**FL**	E	DFIM	LD	
66558	**FL**	E	DFIM	LD	
66559	**FL**	E	DFIM	LD	
66560	**FL**	E	DFIM	LD	
66561	**FL**	E	DFIM	LD	
66562	**FL**	E	DFIM	LD	
66563	**FL**	E	DFIM	LD	
66564	**FL**	E	DFIM	LD	
66565	**FL**	E	DFIM	LD	
66566	**FL**	E	DFIM	LD	
66567	**FL**	E	DFIM	LD	
66568	**FL**	E	DFIM	LD	
66569	**FL**	E	DFIM	LD	
66570	**FL**	E	DFIM	LD	
66571	**FL**	E	DFIM	LD	
66572	**FL**	E	DFIM	LD	

Class 66/5. Freightliner-operated low emission locomotives. Details as Class 66/3.

66585	**FL**	E	DFIN	LD	
66587	**AL**	E	DFIN	LD	AS ONE, WE CAN
66588	**FL**	E	DFIN	LD	
66589	**FL**	E	DHLT	LD (S)	

66590	**FL**	E	DFIN	LD	
66591	**FL**	E	DFIN	LD	
66592	**FL**	E	DFIN	LD	Johnson Stevens Agencies
66593	**FL**	E	DFIN	LD	3MG MERSEY MULTIMODAL GATEWAY
66594	**FL**	E	DFIN	LD	NYK Spirit of Kyoto
66596	**FL**	BN	DFIN	LD	
66597	**FL**	BN	DFIN	LD	Viridor
66598	**FL**	BN	DFIN	LD	
66599	**FL**	BN	DFIN	LD	

Class 66/6. Freightliner-operated locomotives with modified gear ratios.
Details as Class 66/0 except:

Maximum Tractive Effort: 467 kN (105080 lbf).
Continuous Tractive Effort: 296 kN (66630 lbf) at 14.0 mph.
Design Speed: 65 mph.   **Maximum Speed:** 65 mph.

66601	**FL**	P	DFHH	LD	The Hope Valley
66602	**FL**	P	DFHH	LD	
66603	**FL**	P	DFHH	LD	
66604	**FL**	P	DHLT	CB (S)	
66605	**FL**	P	DFHH	LD	
66606	**FL**	P	DFHH	LD	
66607	**FL**	P	DFHH	LD	
66610	**FL**	P	DFHH	LD	
66613	**FL**	E	DFHH	LD	
66614	**FL**	E	DFHH	LD	1916 POPPY 2016
66615	**FL**	E	DFHH	LD	
66616	**FL**	E	DFHH	LD	
66617	**FL**	E	DFHH	LD	
66618	**FL**	E	DFHH	LD	Railways Illustrated Annual Photographic Awards Alan Barnes Derek W. Johnson MBE
66619	**FL**	E	DFHH	LD	
66620	**FL**	E	DFHH	LD	
66621	**FL**	E	DFHH	LD	
66622	**FL**	E	DFHH	LD	

Class 66/6. Freightliner-operated low emission locomotive with modified gear ratios. Details as Class 66/6 except:

Fuel Capacity: 5150 litres.

| 66623 | **FG** | AK | DFHH | LD | |

Class 66/7. Standard design. GB Railfreight-operated locomotives. Details as Class 66/0 exceot 66793 and 66794 which are as Class 66/6.

66701	**GB**	E	GBBT	RR	
66702	**GB**	E	GBBT	RR	Blue Lightning
66703	**GB**	E	GBBT	RR	Doncaster PSB 1981–2002
66704	**GB**	E	GBBT	RR	Colchester Power Signalbox
66705	**GB**	E	GBBT	RR	Golden Jubilee
66706	**GB**	E	GBBT	RR	Nene Valley
66707	**GB**	E	GBBT	RR	Sir Sam Fay GREAT CENTRAL RAILWAY
66708	**GB**	E	GBBT	RR	Jayne

66709	**AL**	E	GBBT	RR	Sorrento
66710	**GB**	E	GBBT	RR	Phil Packer BRIT
66711	**AI**	E	GBBT	RR	Sence
66712	**GB**	E	GBBT	RR	Peterborough Power Signalbox
66713	**GB**	E	GBBT	RR	Forest City
66714	**GB**	E	GBBT	RR	Cromer Lifeboat
66715	**GB**	E	GBBT	RR	VALOUR – IN MEMORY OF ALL RAILWAY EMPLOYEES WHO GAVE THEIR LIVES FOR THEIR COUNTRY
66716	**GB**	E	GBBT	RR	LOCOMOTIVE & CARRIAGE INSTITUTION CENTENARY 1911–2011
66717	**GB**	E	GBBT	RR	Good Old Boy

66718–751. GB Railfreight locomotives.

Details as Class 66/0 except 66718–732/747–749 as below:

Engine: EMD 12N-710G3B-T2 two stroke of 2420 kW (3245 hp) at 904 rpm.
Traction Motors: General Motors D43TRC.
Fuel Capacity: 5546 litres (66718–722) or 5150 litres (66723–732/747–749).

66747–749 were originally built for Crossrail AG in the Netherlands.

66750/751 were originally built for mainland Europe in 2003.

66718	**AL**	E	GBLT	RR	Sir Peter Hendy CBE
66719	**GB**	E	GBLT	RR	METRO-LAND
66720	**0**	E	GBLT	RR	
66721	**AL**	E	GBLT	RR	Harry Beck
66722	**GB**	E	GBLT	RR	Sir Edward Watkin
66723	**GB**	E	GBLT	RR	Chinook
66724	**GB**	E	GBLT	RR	Drax Power Station
66725	**GB**	E	GBLT	RR	SUNDERLAND
66726	**GB**	E	GBLT	RR	SHEFFIELD WEDNESDAY
66727	**MT**	E	GBLT	RR	Maritime One
66728	**GB**	P	GBLT	RR	Institution of Railway Operators
66729	**GB**	P	GBLT	RR	DERBY COUNTY
66730	**GB**	P	GBLT	RR	Whitemoor
66731	**AL**	P	GBLT	RR	Capt. Tom Moore A True British Inspiration
66732	**GB**	P	GBLT	RR	GBRf The First Decade 1999–2009 John Smith – MD

66733	(66401) r	**GB**	P	GBFM	RR	Cambridge PSB
66735	(66403)	**GB**	P	GBBT	RR	PETERBOROUGH UNITED
66736	(66404) r	**GB**	P	GBFM	RR	WOLVERHAMPTON WANDERERS
66737	(66405) r	**GB**	P	GBFM	RR	Lesia
66738	(66578) r	**GB**	BN	GBBT	RR	HUDDERSFIELD TOWN
66739	(66579) r	**GB**	BN	GBFM	RR	Bluebell Railway
66740	(66580) r	**GB**	BN	GBFM	RR	Sarah
66741	(66581)	**GB**	BN	GBBT	RR	Swanage Railway
66742	(66406, 66841)	**GB**	BN	GBBT	RR	ABP Port of Immingham Centenary 1912–2012
66743	(66407, 66842) r	**M**	BN	GBFM	RR	

66744	(66408, 66843)	**GB**	BN	GBBT	RR	Crossrail
66745	(66409, 66844)	**GB**	BN	GBRT	RR	Modern Railways The first 50 years
66746	(66410, 66845) r	**M**	BN	GBFM	RR	
66747	(20078968-007)	**AL**	BN	GBEB	RR	Made in Sheffield
66748	(20078968-004)	**GB**	BN	GBEB	RR	West Burton 50
66749	(20078968-006)	**GB**	BN	GBEB	RR	Christopher Hopcroft MBE 60 Years Railway Service
66750	(20038513-01)	**GB**	BN	GBEB	RR	Bristol Panel Signal Box
66751	(20038513-04) c	**GB**	BN	GBEB	RR	Inspiration Delivered Hitachi Rail Europe

66752–779. Low emission. New build locomotives. Details as Class 66/3.

66752	**GB**	GB	GBEL	RR	The Hoosier State
66753	**GB**	GB	GBEL	RR	EMD Roberts Road
66754	**GB**	GB	GBEL	RR	Northampton Saints
66755	**GB**	GB	GBEL	RR	Tony Berkeley OBE RFG Chairman 1997–2018
66756	**GB**	GB	GBEL	RR	Royal Corps of Signals
66757	**GB**	GB	GBEL	RR	West Somerset Railway
66758	**GB**	GB	GBEL	RR	The Pavior
66759	**GB**	GB	GBEL	RR	Chippy
66760	**GB**	GB	GBEL	RR	David Gordon Harris
66761	**GB**	GB	GBEL	RR	Wensleydale Railway Association 25 Years 1990–2015
66762	**GB**	GB	GBEL	RR	
66763	**GB**	GB	GBEL	RR	Severn Valley Railway
66764	**GB**	GB	GBEL	RR	
66765	**GB**	GB	GBEL	RR	
66766	**GB**	GB	GBEL	RR	
66767	**GB**	GB	GBEL	RR	
66768	**GB**	GB	GBEL	RR	
66769	**GB**	GB	GBEL	RR	
66770	**GB**	GB	GBEL	RR	
66771	**GB**	GB	GBEL	RR	Amanda
66772	**GB**	GB	GBEL	RR	Maria
66773	**GB**	GB	GBNB	RR	Pride of GB Railfreight
66774	**GB**	GB	GBNB	RR	
66775	**GB**	GB	GBNB	RR	HMS Argyll
66776	**GB**	GB	GBNB	RR	Joanne
66777	**GB**	GB	GBNB	RR	Annette
66778	**GB**	GB	GBNB	RR	Cambois Depot 25 Years
66779	**0**	GB	GBEL	RR	EVENING STAR

66780–789. Standard design. Former DB Cargo locomotives acquired by GB Railfreight in 2017. Details as Class 66/0. Fitted with Swinghead Automatic "Buckeye" Combination Couplers.

† Fitted with additional lights and drawgear formerly used for Lickey banking duties.

66780	(66008)	**AL**	GB	GBOB	RR	The Cemex Express

66781	(66016)	**GB**	GB	GBOB	RR
66782	(66046)	**GB**	GB	GBOB	RR
66783	(66058) †	**AL**	GB	GBOB	RR	The Flying Dustman
66784	(66081)	**GB**	GB	GBOB	RR	Keighley & Worth Valley Railway 50th Anniversary 1968–2018
66785	(66132)	**GB**	GB	GBOB	RR
66786	(66141)	**GB**	GB	GBOB	RR
66787	(66184)	**GB**	GB	GBOB	RR
66788	(66238)	**GB**	GB	GBOB	RR	LOCOMOTION 15
66789	(66250)	**BL**	GB	GBOB	RR	British Rail 1948–1997
66790	(T66403)	**GB**	BN	MBDL	RR
66791	(T66404)	**0**	BN	MBDL	RR	Neil Bennett
66792	(T66405)	**GB**	BN	MBDL	RR
66793	(29004)	**0**	BN	MBDL	RR (S) Dave Meehan
66794	(29005)	**0**	BN	MBDL	RR (S) Ted Gaffney
66795			BN		
66796			BN		
66797			BN		

Class 66/8. Standard design. Colas Rail locomotives. Details as Class 66/0.

66846	(66573)	**CS**	BN	COLO	HJ
66847	(66574)	**CS**	BN	COLO	HJ	Terry Baker
66848	(66575)	**CS**	BN	COLO	HJ
66849	(66576)	**CS**	BN	COLO	HJ	Wylam Dilly
66850	(66577)	**CS**	BN	COLO	HJ	David Maidment OBE

Class 66/9. Freightliner locomotives. Low emission "demonstrator" locomotives. Details as Class 66/3. * **Fuel Capacity:** 5905 litres.

66951	*	**FL**	E	DFIN	LD
66952		**FL**	E	DFIN	LD

Class 66/5. Freightliner-operated low emission locomotives. Owing to the 665xx number range being full, subsequent deliveries of 66/5s were numbered from 66953 onwards. Details as Class 66/5 (low emission).

66953	**FL**	BN	DFIN	LD
66955	**FL**	BN	DFIN	LD
66956	**FL**	BN	DFIN	LD
66957	**FL**	BN	DFIN	LD	Stephenson Locomotive Society 1909–2009

CLASS 67   ALSTOM/GENERAL MOTORS   Bo-Bo

Built: 1999–2000 by Alstom at Valencia, Spain, as sub-contractors for General Motors (General Motors model JT42 HW-HS).
Engine: GM 12N-710G3B-EC two stroke of 2385 kW (3200 hp) at 904 rpm.
Main Alternator: General Motors AR9A/HEP7/CA6C.
Traction Motors: General Motors D43FM.
Maximum Tractive Effort: 141 kN (31770 lbf).
Continuous Tractive Effort: 90 kN (20200 lbf) at 46.5 mph.
Power at Rail: 1860 kW.   **Train Brakes:** Air.

Brake Force: 78 t.
Weight: 90 t.
Design Speed: 125 mph.
Fuel Capacity: 4927 litres.
Train Supply: Electric, index 66.

Dimensions: 19.74 x 2.72 m.
Wheel Diameter: 965 mm.
Maximum Speed: 125 mph.
Route Availability: 8.
Total: 30.

All equipped with Slow Speed Control and Swinghead Automatic "Buckeye" Combination Couplers.

The following locomotives have been modified to operate with TfW Mark 4 stock: 67008, 67010, 67014, 67015, 67017, 67025.

Non-standard liveries:

67026 Diamond Jubilee silver.
67029 All over silver with DB logos.

67001	**AB**	DB	WAAC	CE	
67002	**AB**	DB	WAAC	CE	
67003	**AB**	DB	WQBA	TO (S)	
67004 r	**DB**	DB	WQAB	TO (S)	
67005	**RZ**	DB	WAAC	CE	Queen's Messenger
67006	**RZ**	DB	WAAC	CE	Royal Sovereign
67007 r	**E**	DB	WAAC	CE	
67008	**TW**	DB	WACC	CE	
67009 r	**E**	DB	WQBA	CE (S)	
67010	**DB**	DB	WAAC	CE	
67011 r	**E**	DB	WQBA	CE (S)	
67012	**CM**	DB	WAAC	CE	
67013	**DB**	DB	WAAC	CE	
67014	**TW**	DB	WACC	CE	
67015	**DB**	DB	WAAC	CE	
67016	**E**	DB	WAAC	CE	
67017	**TW**	DB	WACC	CE	
67018	**DB**	DB	WQBA	CE (S)	Keith Heller
67019	**E**	DB	WQBA	TO (S)	
67020	**E**	DB	WAAC	CE	
67021	**PC**	DB	WAAC	CE	
67022	**E**	DB	WQBA	CE (S)	
67023	**CS**	BN	COTS	RU	Stella
67024	**PC**	DB	WAAC	CE	
67025	**TW**	DB	WACC	TO	
67026	**0**	DB	WQBA	CE (S)	Diamond Jubilee
67027	**CS**	BN	COTS	RU	Charlotte
67028	**DB**	DB	WAAC	CE	
67029	**0**	DB	WQAA	CE (S)	Royal Diamond
67030 r	**E**	DB	WQAA	CE (S)	

CLASS 68   VOSSLOH/STADLER   Bo-Bo

New Vossloh/Stadler mixed-traffic locomotives operated by DRS.

Built: 2012–16 by Vossloh/Stadler, Valencia, Spain.
Engine: Caterpillar C175-16 of 2800 kW (3750 hp) at 1740 rpm.

Main Alternator: ABB WGX560.
Traction Motors: 4 x AMXL400 AC frame mounted ABB 4FRA6063.
Maximum Tractive Effort: 317 kN (71260 lbf).
Continuous Tractive Effort: 258 kN (58000 lbf) at 20.5 mph.

Power at Rail:	**Train Brakes:** Air & rheostatic.
Brake Force: 73 t.	**Dimensions:** 20.50 x 2.69 m.
Weight: 85 t.	**Wheel Diameter:** 1100 mm.
Design Speed: 100 mph.	**Maximum Speed:** 100 mph.
Fuel Capacity: 5600 litres.	**Route Availability:** 7.
Train Supply: Electric, index 96.	**Total:** 34.

68008–015 have been modified to operate in push-pull mode on the Chiltern Railways locomotive-hauled sets.

68019–034 have been modified to operate with the TransPennine Express Mark 5A stock.

68001	DI	BN	XHVE	CR	Evolution
68002	DI	BN	XHVE	CR	Intrepid
68003	DI	BN	XHVE	CR	Astute
68004	DI	BN	XHVE	CR	Rapid
68005	DI	BN	XHVE	CR	Defiant
68006	SR	BN	XHVE	CR	Daring
68007	SR	BN	XHVE	CR	Valiant
68008	DI	BN	XHVE	CR	Avenger
68009	DI	BN	XHVE	CR	Titan
68010	CM	BN	XHCE	CR	Oxford Flyer
68011	CM	BN	XHCE	CR	
68012	CM	BN	XHCE	CR	
68013	CM	BN	XHCE	CR	
68014	CM	BN	XHCE	CR	
68015	CM	BN	XHCE	CR	
68016	DI	BN	XHVE	CR	Fearless
68017	DI	BN	XHVE	CR	Hornet
68018	DI	BN	XHVE	CR	Vigilant
68019	TP	BN	TPEX	CR	Brutus
68020	TP	BN	TPEX	CR	Reliance
68021	TP	BN	TPEX	CR	Tireless
68022	TP	BN	TPEX	CR	Resolution
68023	TP	BN	TPEX	CR	Achilles
68024	TP	BN	TPEX	CR	Centaur
68025	TP	BN	TPEX	CR	Superb
68026	TP	BN	TPEX	CR	Enterprise
68027	TP	BN	TPEX	CR	Splendid
68028	TP	BN	TPEX	CR	Lord President
68029	TP	BN	TPEX	CR	Courageous
68030	TP	BN	TPEX	CR	Black Douglas
68031	TP	BN	TPEX	CR	Felix
68032	TP	BN	TPEX	CR	Destroyer
68033	DI	DR	XHVE	CR	
68034	DI	DR	XHVE	CR	

CLASS 69   BRUSH/BR/RUSTON/EMD   Co-Co

These locomotives are heavy rebuilds of Class 56s for GB Railfreight, with new General Motors engines, the same type as used in the Class 66s. The first rebuild is due to be completed in February 2021 and it is planned that a total of 16 locomotives will be rebuilt. Full details awaited. Donor locomotives are provisional.

Built: 1976–84 by Electroputere at Craiova, Romania (as sub-contractors for Brush) or BREL at Doncaster or Crewe Works. Rebuilt 2019–21 by ElectroMotive Diesel Services, Longport.
Engine: General Motors 12N-710G3B-T2 two stroke of 2385 kW (3200 hp) at 904 rpm.
Main Alternator:
Traction Motors:
Maximum Tractive Effort:
Continuous Tractive Effort:
Power at Rail: **Train Brakes:** Air.
Brake Force: **Dimensions:** 19.36 x 2.79 m.
Weight: **Wheel Diameter:**
Design Speed: **Maximum Speed:**
Fuel Capacity: **Route Availability:**
Train Supply: Not equipped.

69001	(56311)	GB
69002	(56031)	GB
69003	(56018)	GB
69004		GB
69005		GB
69006		GB
69007		GB
69008		GB
69009		GB
69010		GB
69011		GB
69012		GB
69013		GB
69014		GB
69015		GB
69016		GB

CLASS 70   GENERAL ELECTRIC   Co-Co

GE "PowerHaul" locomotives. 70012 was badly damaged whilst being unloaded in 2011 and was returned to Pennsylvania.

70801 (built as 70099) is a Turkish-built demonstrator that arrived in Britain in 2012. Colas Rail leased this locomotive and then in 2013 ordered a further nine locomotives (70802–810) that were delivered in 2014. 70811–817 followed in 2017.

Built: 2009–17 by General Electric, Erie, Pennsylvania, USA or by TÜLOMSAS, Eskişehir, Turkey (70801).

Engine: General Electric PowerHaul P616LDA1 of 2848 kW (3820 hp) at 1500 rpm.
Main Alternator: General Electric GTA series.
Traction Motors: AC-GE 5GEB30.
Maximum Tractive Effort: 544 kN (122000 lbf).
Continuous Tractive Effort: 427 kN (96000 lbf) at 11 mph.
Power at Rail: **Train Brakes:** Air.
Brake Force: 96.7 t.   **Dimensions:** 21.71 x 2.64 m.
Weight: 129 t.   **Wheel Diameter:** 1066 mm.
Design Speed: 75 mph.   **Maximum Speed:** 75 mph.
Fuel Capacity: 6000 litres.   **Route Availability:** 7.
Train Supply: Not equipped.   **Total:** 36.

Class 70/0. Freightliner locomotives.

70001	**FH**	AK	DFGI	LD	PowerHaul
70002	**FH**	AK	DHLT	LD (S)	
70003	**FH**	AK	DFGI	LD	
70004	**FH**	AK	DHLT	LD (S)	The Coal Industry Society
70005	**FH**	AK	DFGI	LD	
70006	**FH**	AK	DHLT	CB (S)	
70007	**FH**	AK	DFGI	LD	
70008	**FH**	AK	DFGI	LD	
70009	**FH**	AK	DHLT	LD (S)	
70010	**FH**	AK	DFGI	LD	
70011	**FH**	AK	DHLT	CB (S)	
70013	**FH**	AK	DHLT	LD (S)	
70014	**FH**	AK	DHLT	CB (S)	
70015	**FH**	AK	DFGI	LD	
70016	**FH**	AK	DFGI	LD	
70017	**FH**	AK	DFGI	LD	
70018	**FH**	AK	DHLT	LD (S)	
70019	**FH**	AK	DHLT	LD (S)	
70020	**FH**	AK	DFGI	LD	

Class 70/8. Colas Rail locomotives.

70801	**CS**	LF	COLO	CF
70802	**CS**	LF	COLO	CF
70803	**CS**	LF	COLO	CF
70804	**CS**	LF	COLO	CF
70805	**CS**	LF	COLO	CF
70806	**CS**	LF	COLO	CF
70807	**CS**	LF	COLO	CF
70808	**CS**	LF	COLO	CF
70809	**CS**	LF	COLO	CF
70810	**CS**	LF	COLO	CF
70811	**CS**	BN	COLO	CF
70812	**CS**	BN	COLO	CF
70813	**CS**	BN	COLO	CF
70814	**CS**	BN	COLO	CF
70815	**CS**	BN	COLO	CF
70816	**CS**	BN	COLO	CF
70817	**CS**	BN	COLO	CF

2. ELECTRO-DIESEL & ELECTRIC LOCOMOTIVES

CLASS 73/1   BR/ENGLISH ELECTRIC   Bo-Bo

Electro-diesel locomotives which can operate either from a DC supply or using power from a diesel engine.

Built: 1965–67 by English Electric Co. at Vulcan Foundry, Newton-le-Willows.
Engine: English Electric 4SRKT of 447 kW (600 hp) at 850 rpm.
Main Generator: English Electric 824/5D.
Electric Supply System: 750 V DC from third rail.
Traction Motors: English Electric 546/1B.
Maximum Tractive Effort (Electric): 179 kN (40000 lbf).
Maximum Tractive Effort (Diesel): 160 kN (36000 lbf).
Continuous Rating (Electric): 1060 kW (1420 hp) giving a tractive effort of 35 kN (7800 lbf) at 68 mph.
Continuous Tractive Effort (Diesel): 60 kN (13600 lbf) at 11.5 mph.
Maximum Rail Power (Electric): 2350 kW (3150 hp) at 42 mph.
Train Brakes: Air, vacuum & electro-pneumatic († Air & electro-pneumatic).
Brake Force: 31 t.   **Dimensions:** 16.36 x 2.64 m.
Weight: 77 t.   **Wheel Diameter:** 1016 mm.
Design Speed: 90 mph.   **Maximum Speed:** 90 mph.
Fuel Capacity: 1409 litres.   **Route Availability:** 6.
Train Supply: Electric, index 66 (on electric power only). **Total:** 30.

Formerly numbered E6007–E6020/E6022–E6026/E6028–E6049 (not in order).

Locomotives numbered in the 732xx series are classed as 73/2 and were originally dedicated to Gatwick Express services.

There have been two separate Class 73 rebuild projects. For GBRf 11 locomotives were rebuilt at Brush, Loughborough with a 1600 hp MTU engine (renumbered 73961–971). For Network Rail 73104/211 were rebuilt at RVEL Derby (now Loram) with 2 x QSK19 750 hp engines (73951/952).

Non-standard liveries and numbering:

73110   Carries original number E6016.
73128   Two-tone grey.
73139   Light blue & light grey.
73235   Plain dark blue.

73101	**PC**	GB	GBSD	ZG (S)	
73107	**GB**	GB	GBED	SE	Tracy
73109	**GB**	GB	GBED	SE	Battle of Britain 80th Anniversary
73110	**B**	GB	GBBR	ZG (S)	
73119	**GB**	GB	GBED	SE	Borough of Eastleigh
73128	**GB**	GB	GBED	SE	O.V.S. BULLEID C.B.E.
73133	**TT**	TT	MBED	ZG	
73134	**IC**	GB	GBBR	LB (S)	Woking Homes 1885–1985

73136	**GB**	GB	GBED	SE	Mhairi
73138	**Y**	NR	QADD	ZA	
73139	**0**	GB	GBSD	ZG (S)	
73141	**GB**	GB	GBED	SE	Charlotte
73201 †	**B**	GB	GBED	SE	Broadlands
73202 †	**SN**	P	MBED	SL	Graham Stenning
73212 †	**GB**	GB	GBED	SE	Fiona
73213 †	**GB**	GB	GBED	SE	Rhodalyn
73235 †	**0**	P	HYWD	BM	

CLASS 73/9 (RVEL)   BR/RVEL   Bo-Bo

The 7395x number series is reserved for rebuilt Network Rail locomotives.

Rebuilt: Re-engineered by RVEL Derby 2013–15.
Engine: 2 x QSK19 of 560 kW (750 hp) at 1800 rpm (total 1120 kw (1500 hp)).
Main Alternator: 2 x Marathon Magnaplus.
Electric Supply System: 750 V DC from third rail.
Traction Motors: English Electric 546/1B.
Maximum Tractive Effort (Electric): 179 kN (40000 lbf).
Maximum Tractive Effort (Diesel): 179 kN (40000 lbf).
Continuous Rating (Electric): 1060 kW (1420 hp) giving a tractive effort of 35kN (7800 lbf) at 68 mph.
Continuous Tractive Effort (Diesel): 990 kW (1328 hp) giving a tractive effort of 33kN (7420 lbf) at 68 mph.
Maximum Rail Power (Electric): 2350 kW (3150 hp) at 42 mph.

Train Brakes: Air.	**Brake Force:** 31 t.
Weight: 77 t.	**Dimensions:** 16.36 x 2.64 m.
Maximum Speed: 90 mph.	**Wheel Diameter:** 1016 mm.
Fuel Capacity: 2260 litres.	**Route Availability:** 6.
Train Supply: Not equipped.	

| 73951 (73104) | **Y** | LO | QADD | ZA | Malcolm Brinded |
| 73952 (73211) | **Y** | LO | QADD | ZA | Janis Kong |

CLASS 73/9 (GBRf)   BR/BRUSH   Bo-Bo

GBRf Class 73s rebuilt at Brush Loughborough. 73961–965 are normally used on Network Rail contracts and 73966–971 are used by Caledonian Sleeper.

Rebuilt: Re-engineered by Brush, Loughborough 2014–16.
Engine: MTU 8V4000 R43L of 1195 kW (1600 hp) at 1800 rpm.
Main Alternator: Lechmotoren SDV 87.53-12.
Electric Supply System: 750 V DC from third rail (73961–965 only).
Traction Motors: English Electric 546/1B.
Maximum Tractive Effort (Electric): 179 kN (40000 lbf).
Maximum Tractive Effort (Diesel): 179 kN (40000 lbf).
Continuous Rating (Electric): 1060 kW (1420 hp) giving a tractive effort of 35kN (7800 lbf) at 68 mph.
Continuous Tractive Effort (Diesel):

Maximum Rail Power (Electric): 2350 kW (3150 hp) at 42 mph.
Train Brakes: Air.   **Brake Force:** 31 t.
Weight: 77 t.   **Dimensions:** 16.36 x 2.64 m.
Maximum Speed: 90 mph.   **Wheel Diameter:** 1016 mm.
Fuel Capacity: 1409 litres.   **Route Availability:** 6.
Train Supply: Electric, index 38 (electric & diesel).

73961	(73209)	**GB** GB	GBNR	SE	Alison
73962	(73204)	**GB** GB	GBNR	SE	Dick Mabbutt
73963	(73206)	**GB** GB	GBNR	SE	Janice
73964	(73205)	**GB** GB	GBNR	SE	Jeanette
73965	(73208)	**GB** GB	GBNR	SE	

73966–971 have been rebuilt for Caledonian Sleeper but their third rail electric capability has been retained. They have a higher Train Supply index and a slightly higher fuel capacity. Details as 73961–965 except:
Fuel Capacity: 1509 litres.   **Train Supply:** Electric, index 96.

73005 and 73006 were originally assembled at Eastleigh Works.

73966	(73005)	d **CA** GB	GBCS	EC
73967	(73006)	d **CA** GB	GBCS	EC
73968	(73117)	d **CA** GB	GBCS	EC
73969	(73105)	d **CA** GB	GBCS	EC
73970	(73103)	d **CA** GB	GBCS	EC
73971	(73207)	d **CA** GB	GBCS	EC

CLASS 86   BR/ENGLISH ELECTRIC   Bo-Bo

Built: 1965–66 by English Electric Co at Vulcan Foundry, Newton-le-Willows or by BR at Doncaster Works.
Electric Supply System: 25 kV AC 50 Hz overhead.
Traction Motors: AEI 282BZ axle hung.
Maximum Tractive Effort: 207 kN (46500 lbf).
Continuous Rating: 3010 kW (4040 hp) giving a tractive effort of 85kN (19200lbf) at 77.5 mph.
Maximum Rail Power: 4550 kW (6100 hp) at 49.5 mph.
Train Brakes: Air.   **Brake Force:** 40 t.
Dimensions: 17.83 x 2.65 m.   **Weight:** 83–86.8 t.
Wheel Diameter: 1156 mm.   **Train Supply:** Electric, index 74.
Design Speed: 110–125 mph.   **Maximum Speed:** 100 mph.
Route Availability: 6.   **Total:** 21.

Formerly numbered E3101–E3200 (not in order).

Class 86s exported for use abroad are listed in section 5 of this book.

Class 86/1. Class 87-type bogies & motors. Details as above except:

Traction Motors: GEC 412AZ frame mounted.
Maximum Tractive Effort: 258 kN (58000 lbf).
Continuous Rating: 3730 kW (5000 hp) giving a tractive effort of 95kN (21300lbf) at 87 mph.
Maximum Rail Power: 5860 kW (7860 hp) at 50.8 mph.

Wheel Diameter: 1150 mm.
Design Speed: 110 mph.   **Maximum Speed:** 110 mph.

| 86101 | **IC** | LS | LSLO | CL | Sir William A Stanier FRS |

Class 86/2. Standard design rebuilt with resilient wheels & Flexicoil suspension. Details as in main class heading.

Non-standard livery:

86259 BR "Electric blue". Also carries number E3137.

| 86251 | **V** | FL | EPEX | CB (S) | |
| 86259 x | **0** | PP | MBEL | WN | Les Ross/Peter Pan |

Class 86/4. Details as Class 86/2 except:

Traction Motors: AEI 282AZ axle hung.
Maximum Tractive Effort: 258 kN (58000 lbf).
Continuous Rating: 2680 kW (3600 hp) giving a tractive effort of 89 kN (20000 lbf) at 67 mph.
Maximum Rail Power: 4400 kW (5900 hp) at 38 mph.
Weight: 83–83.9 t.
Design Speed: 100 mph.   **Maximum Speed:** 100 mph.

| 86401 | **CA** | WC | GBCH | WN | Mons Meg |

Class 86/6. Freightliner-operated locomotives.

Previously numbered in the Class 86/0 and 86/4 series'. 86608 was also regeared and renumbered 86501 between 2000 and 2016.

Details as Class 86/4 except:
Traction Motors: AEI 282AZ axle hung.
Maximum Speed: 75 mph.   **Train Supply:** Electric, isolated.

86604	**FL**	FL	DFNC	CB
86605	**FL**	FL	DHLT	CB (S)
86607	**FL**	FL	DFNC	CB
86608	**FL**	FL	DFNC	CB
86609	**FL**	FL	DFNC	CB
86610	**FL**	FL	DHLT	CB (S)
86612	**FL**	FL	DHLT	CB (S)
86613	**FL**	FL	DFNC	CB
86614	**FL**	FL	DHLT	CB (S)
86622	**FH**	FL	DFNC	CB
86627	**FL**	FL	DHLT	CB (S)
86628	**FL**	FL	DHLT	CB (S)
86632	**FL**	FL	DFNC	CB
86637	**FH**	FL	DFNC	CB
86638	**FL**	FL	DFNC	CB
86639	**FL**	FL	DFNC	CB

CLASS 87   BREL/GEC   Bo-Bo

Built: 1973–75 by BREL at Crewe Works.
Electric Supply System: 25 kV AC 50 Hz overhead.
Traction Motors: GEC G412AZ frame mounted.
Maximum Tractive Effort: 258 kN (58000 lbf).
Continuous Rating: 3730 kW (5000 hp) giving a tractive effort of 95 kN
(21300lbf) at 87 mph.
Maximum Rail Power: 5860 kW (7860 hp) at 50.8 mph.
Train Brakes: Air.   **Brake Force:** 40 t.
Dimensions: 17.83 x 2.65 m.   **Weight:** 83.3 t.
Wheel Diameter: 1150 mm.   **Train Supply:** Electric, index 95.
Design Speed: 110 mph.   **Maximum Speed:** 110 mph.
Route Availability: 6.   **Total:** 1.

Class 87s exported for use abroad are listed in section 5 of this book.

| 87002 | **IC** | LS | LSLO | CL | Royal Sovereign |

CLASS 88   VOSSLOH/STADLER   Bo-Bo

New Vossloh/Stadler bi-mode DRS locomotives.

Built: 2015–16 by Vossloh/Sladler, Valencia, Spain.
Electric Supply System: 25 kV AC 50 Hz overhead.
Engine: Caterpillar C27 12-cylinder 708 kW (950 hp) at 1750 rpm.
Main Alternator: ABB AMXL400.
Traction Motors: ABB AMXL400.
Maximum Tractive Effort (Electric): 317 kN (71 260 lbf).
Maximum Tractive Effort (Diesel): 317 kN (71 260 lbf).
Continuous Rating: 4000 kW (5360 hp) giving a tractive effort of 258 kN
(58000 lbf) at 28 mph (electric).
Maximum Rail Power:
Train Brakes: Air, regenerative & rheostatic.
Brake Force: 73 t.   **Dimensions:** 20.50 x 2.69 m.
Weight: 85 t.   **Wheel Diameter:** 1100 mm.
Fuel Capacity: 1800 litres.   **Train Supply:** Electric, index 96.
Design Speed: 100 mph.   **Maximum Speed:** 100 mph.
Route Availability: 7.   **Total:** 10.

88001	**DI**	BN	XHVE	KM	Revolution
88002	**DI**	BN	XHVE	KM	Prometheus
88003	**DI**	BN	XHVE	KM	Genesis
88004	**DI**	BN	XHVE	KM	Pandora
88005	**DI**	BN	XHVE	KM	Minerva
88006	**DI**	BN	XHVE	KM	Juno
88007	**DI**	BN	XHVE	KM	Electra
88008	**DI**	BN	XHVE	KM	Ariadne
88009	**DI**	BN	XHVE	KM	Diana
88010	**DI**	BN	XHVE	KM	Aurora

CLASS 90   GEC   Bo-Bo

Built: 1987–90 by BREL at Crewe Works (as sub-contractors for GEC).
Electric Supply System: 25 kV AC 50 Hz overhead.
Traction Motors: GEC G412CY frame mounted.
Maximum Tractive Effort: 258 kN (58000 lbf).
Continuous Rating: 3730 kW (5000 hp) giving a tractive effort of 95 kN (21300 lbf) at 87 mph.
Maximum Rail Power: 5860 kW (7860 hp) at 68.3 mph.

Train Brakes: Air.	**Dimensions:** 18.80 x 2.74 m.
Brake Force: 40 t.	**Wheel Diameter:** 1150 mm.
Weight: 84.5 t.	**Maximum Speed:** 110 mph.
Design Speed: 110 mph.	**Route Availability:** 7.
Train Supply: Electric, index 95.	**Total:** 50.

Advertising livery: 90024 Malcolm Logistics (blue).

90001	b	**IC**	LS	LSLO	CL	Royal Scot
90002	b	**IC**	LS	LSLO	CL	Wolf of Badenoch
90003	b	**GA**	FL	DFLC	CB	
90004	b	**GA**	FL	DFLC	CB	City of Chelmsford
90005	b	**GA**	FL	DFLC	CB	Vice-Admiral Lord Nelson
90006	b	**GA**	FL	DFLC	CB	Modern Railways Magazine/ Roger Ford
90007	b	**GA**	FL	DFLC	CB	Sir John Betjeman
90008	b	**GA**	FL	DFLC	CB	The East Anglian
90009	b	**GA**	FL	DFLC	CB	
90010	b	**GA**	FL	DFLC	CB	
90011	b	**GA**	FL	DFLC	CB	East Anglian Daily Times Suffolk & Proud
90012	b	**GA**	FL	DFLC	CB	Royal Anglian Regiment
90013	b	**GA**	FL	DFLC	CB	
90014	b	**FG**	FL	DFLC	CB	Over the Rainbow
90015	b	**GA**	FL	DFLC	CB	Colchester Castle
90016		**FL**	FL	DFLC	CB	
90017		**E**	DB	WQBA	CE (S)	
90018		**DB**	DB	WQAB	CE (S)	The Pride of Bellshill
90019		**DB**	DB	WFMS	CE (S)	Multimodal
90020		**GC**	DB	WEDC	CE	
90021		**FS**	DB	WQAA	CE (S)	
90022		**EG**	DB	WQBA	CE (S)	Freightconnection
90023		**E**	DB	WQBA	CE (S)	
90024		**AL**	DB	WQAB	CE (S)	
90025		**F**	DB	WQBA	CE (S)	
90026		**GC**	DB	WEDC	CE	
90027		**F**	DB	WQBA	CE (S)	Allerton T&RS Depot
90028		**DB**	DB	WEDC	CE	Sir William McAlpine
90029		**GC**	DB	WEDC	CE	
90030		**E**	DB	WQBA	CE (S)	
90031		**E**	DB	WQBA	CE (S)	The Railway Children Partnership Working For Street Children Worldwide
90032		**E**	DB	WQBA	CE (S)	

90033	**FE**	DB	WQBA	CE (S)	
90034	**DR**	DB	WEDC	CE	
90035	**DB**	DB	WEAC	CE	
90036	**DB**	DB	WEDC	CE	Driver Jack Mills
90037	**DB**	DB	WEAC	CE	Christine
90038	**FE**	DB	WQBA	CE (S)	
90039	**E**	DB	WFMS	CE (S)	
90040	**DB**	DB	WQAA	CE (S)	
90041	**FL**	FL	DFLC	CB	
90042	**FH**	FL	DFLC	CB	
90043	**FH**	FL	DFLC	CB	
90044	**FG**	FL	DFLC	CB	
90045	**FH**	FL	DFLC	CB	
90046	**FL**	FL	DFLC	CB	
90047	**FG**	FL	DFLC	CB	
90048	**FF**	FL	DFLC	CB	
90049	**FH**	FL	DFLC	CB	
90050	**FF**	AV	DHLT	CB (S)	

CLASS 91   GEC   Bo-Bo

Built: 1988–91 by BREL at Crewe Works (as sub-contractors for GEC).
Electric Supply System: 25 kV AC 50 Hz overhead.
Traction Motors: GEC G426AZ.
Maximum Tractive Effort: 190 kN (43 000 lbf).
Continuous Rating: 4540 kW (6090 hp) giving a tractive effort of 170 kN at 96 mph.
Maximum Rail Power: 4700 kW (6300 hp) at ?? mph.

Train Brakes: Air.	**Dimensions:** 19.41 x 2.74 m.
Brake Force: 45 t.	**Wheel Diameter:** 1000 mm.
Weight: 84 t.	**Maximum Speed:** 125 mph.
Design Speed: 140 mph.	**Route Availability:** 7.
Train Supply: Electric, index 95.	**Total:** 31.

Locomotives were originally numbered in the 910xx series, but were renumbered upon completion of overhauls at Bombardier, Doncaster by the addition of 100 to their original number. The exception to this rule was 91023 which was renumbered 91132.

91114 has been fitted with a second pantograph for evaluation purposes.

Advertising liveries:

91101 Flying Scotsman (red, white & purple).
91110 Battle of Britain (black and grey).
91111 For the fallen (various with poppy and Union Jack vinyls).

91101	**AL**	E	IECA	BN	FLYING SCOTSMAN
91102	**VE**	E	SAXL	DR (S)	City of York
91103	**VE**	E	SAXL	ZB (S)	
91104	**VE**	E	SAXL	DR (S)	
91105	**VE**	E	IECA	BN	
91106	**VE**	E	IECA	BN	

91107	**VE**	E	IECA	BN	SKYFALL
91108	**VE**	E	SAXL	ZB (S)	
91109	**VE**	E	IECA	BN	Sir Bobby Robson
91110	**AL**	E	IECA	BN	BATTLE OF BRITAIN MEMORIAL FLIGHT
91111	**AL**	E	IECA	BN	For the Fallen
91112	**VE**	E	SAXL	DR (S)	
91113	**VE**	E	SAXL	DR (S)	
91114	**VE**	E	IECA	BN	Durham Cathedral
91115	**VE**	E	SAXL	DR (S)	Blaydon Races
91116	**VE**	E	SAXL	DR (S)	
91117	**EX**	EP	EPEX	LR (S)	
91118	**VE**	E	SAXL	DR (S)	The Fusiliers
91119	**IC**	E	IECA	BN	Bounds Green INTERCITY Depot 1977–2017
91120	**EX**	EP	EPEX	LR (S)	
91121	**VE**	E	SAXL	DR (S)	
91122	**VE**	E	EROG	LR	
91124	**VE**	E	IECA	BN	
91125	**VE**	E	SAXL	DR (S)	
91126	**VE**	E	SAXL	DR (S)	Darlington Hippodrome
91127	**VE**	E	IECA	BN	
91128	**VE**	E	EROG	LR	INTERCITY 50
91129	**VE**	E	SAXL	DR (S)	
91130	**VE**	E	IECA	BN	Lord Mayor of Newcastle
91131	**VE**	E	SAXL	DR (S)	
91132	**VE**	E	SAXL	DR (S)	

CLASS 92   BRUSH   Co-Co

Built: 1993–96 by Brush Traction at Loughborough.
Electric Supply System: 25 kV AC 50 Hz overhead or 750 V DC third rail.
Traction Motors: Asea Brown Boveri design. Model 6FRA 7059B (Asynchronous 3-phase induction motors).
Maximum Tractive Effort: 400 kN (90 000 lbf).
Continuous Rating: 5040 kW (6760 hp) on AC, 4000 kW (5360 hp) on DC.

Maximum Rail Power:	**Train Brakes:** Air.
Brake Force: 63 t.	**Dimensions:** 21.34 x 2.67 m.
Weight: 126 t.	**Wheel Diameter:** 1070 mm.
Design Speed: 140 km/h (87 mph).	**Maximum Speed:** 140 km/h (87 mph).
Train Supply: Electric, index 180 (AC), 108 (DC).	
Route Availability: 7.	**Total:** 33.

* Fitted with TVM430 signalling equipment to operate on High Speed 1.

Class 92s exported for use abroad are listed in section 5 of this book.

Advertising livery: 92017 Stobart Rail (two-tone blue & white).

92004		**EG**	DB	WQBA	CE (S)	Jane Austen
92006	d	**CA**	GB	GBSL	WB	
92007		**EG**	DB	WQBA	CE (S)	Schubert
92008		**EG**	DB	WQBA	CE (S)	Jules Verne
92009	*	**DB**	DB	WQBA	CE (S)	Marco Polo
92010	*d	**CA**	GB	GBST	WB	
92011	*	**EG**	DB	WFBC	CE	Handel
92013		**EG**	DB	WQBA	CE (S)	Puccini
92014	d	**CA**	GB	GBSL	WB	
92015	*	**DB**	DB	WFBC	CE	
92016	*	**DB**	DB	WQBA	CE (S)	
92017		**AL**	DB	WQBA	CE (S)	Bart the Engine
92018	*d	**CA**	GB	GBST	WB	
92019	*	**EG**	DB	WFBC	CE	Wagner
92020	d	**GB**	GB	GBSL	WB	
92021		**EP**	GB	GBSD	LB (S)	Purcell
92023	*d	**CA**	GB	GBSL	WB	
92028	d	**GB**	GB	GBST	WB	
92029		**EG**	DB	WQAB	CE (S)	Dante
92031	*	**DB**	DB	WQBA	CE (S)	
92032	*d	**GB**	GB	GBCT	WB	IMechE Railway Division
92033	d	**CA**	GB	GBSL	WB	
92035		**EG**	DB	WQBA	CE (S)	Mendelssohn
92036	*	**EG**	DB	WFBC	CE	Bertolt Brecht
92037		**EG**	DB	WQBA	CE (S)	Sullivan
92038	*d	**CA**	GB	GBST	WB	
92040		**EP**	GB	GBSD	LB (S)	Goethe
92041	*	**EG**	DB	WFBC	CE	Vaughan Williams
92042	*	**DB**	DB	WFBC	CE	
92043	*d	**GB**	GB	GBST	WB	
92044	*	**EP**	GB	GBCT	WB	Couperin
92045		**EP**	GB	GBSD	LB (S)	Chaucer
92046		**EP**	GB	GBSD	LB (S)	Sweelinck

3. EUROTUNNEL LOCOMOTIVES

DIESEL LOCOMOTIVES

0001–10 are registered on TOPS as 21901–910.

0001–0005   Krupp MaK   Bo-Bo

Channel Tunnel maintenance and rescue train locomotives.
Built: 1991–92 by MaK at Kiel, Germany (Model DE 1004).
Engine: MTU 12V396 TC 13 of 950 kW (1275 hp) at 1800 rpm.
Main Alternator: ABB.   **Traction Motors:** ABB.
Maximum Tractive Effort: 305 kN (68600 lbf).
Continuous Tractive Effort: 140 kN (31500 lbf) at 20 mph.
Power At Rail: 750 kW (1012 hp).   **Dimensions:** 14.40 x ?? m.
Brake Force: 120 kN.   **Wheel Diameter:** 1000 mm.
Train Brakes: Air.   **Weight:** 90 t.
Maximum Speed: 100 km/h.   **Design Speed:** 120 km/h.
Fuel Capacity: 3500 litres.   **Multiple Working:** Within class.
Train Supply: Not equipped.   **Signalling System:** TVM430 cab signalling.

0001	**GY**	ET	CT		0004	**GY**	ET	CT
0002	**GY**	ET	CT		0005	**GY**	ET	CT
0003	**GY**	ET	CT					

0006–0010   Krupp MaK   Bo-Bo

Channel Tunnel maintenance and rescue locomotives. Rebuilt from Netherlands Railways/DB Cargo Nederland Class 6400. 0006/07 were added to the ET fleet in 2011, and 0008–10 in 2016. 0010 is used for shunting at Coquelles.

Built: 1990–91 by MaK at Kiel, Germany (Model DE 6400).
Engine: MTU 12V396 TC 13 of 1180 kW (1580 hp) at 1800 rpm.
Main Alternator: ABB.   **Traction Motors:** ABB.
Maximum Tractive Effort: 290 kN (65200 lbf).
Continuous Tractive Effort: 140 kN (31500 lbf) at 20 mph.
Power At Rail: 750 kW (1012 hp).   **Dimensions:** 14.40 x ?? m.
Brake Force: 120 kN.   **Wheel Diameter:** 1000 mm.
Train Brakes: Air.   **Weight:** 80 t.
Maximum Speed: 120 km/h.   **Design Speed:** 120 km/h.
Fuel Capacity: 2900 litres.   **Multiple Working:** Within class.
Train Supply: Not equipped.

Not fitted with TVM 430 cab signalling so have to operate with another locomotive/s when used on HS1.

0006	(6456)	**GY**	ET	CT		0009	(6451)	**GY**	ET	CT
0007	(6457)	**GY**	ET	CT		0010	(6447)	**EB**	ET	CO
0008	(6450)	**GY**	ET	CT						

0031–0042   HUNSLET/SCHÖMA   0-4-0

Built: 1989–90 by Hunslet Engine Company at Leeds as 900 mm gauge.
Rebuilt: 1993–94 by Schöma in Germany to 1435 mm gauge as Type CFL 200 DCL-R.
Engine: Deutz F10L 413 FW of 170 kW (230 hp) at 2300 rpm.
Transmission: Mechanical Clark 5421-179 type.
Maximum Tractive Effort: 68 kN (15300 lbf).
Continuous Tractive Effort: 47 kN (10570 lbf) at 5 mph.
Power At Rail: 130.1 kW (175 hp).
Brake Force: **Dimensions:** 7.87 (* 10.94) x 2.69 m.
Weight: 25 t. (* 28 t.)   **Wheel Diameter:** 1010 mm.
Maximum Speed: 48 km/h (* 75 km/h).
Fuel Capacity: 450 litres.   **Train Brakes:** Air.
Train Supply: Not equipped.   **Multiple Working:** Not equipped.

* Rebuilt with inspection platforms to check overhead catenary (Type CS 200).

0031		**GY**	ET	CT	FRANCES
0032		**GY**	ET	CT	ELISABETH
0033		**GY**	ET	CT	SILKE
0034		**GY**	ET	CT	AMANDA
0035		**GY**	ET	CT	MARY
0036		**GY**	ET	CT	LAURENCE
0037		**GY**	ET	CT	LYDIE
0038		**GY**	ET	CT	JENNY
0039	*	**GY**	ET	CT	PACITA
0040		**GY**	ET	CT	JILL
0041	*	**GY**	ET	CT	KIM
0042		**GY**	ET	CT	NICOLE

ELECTRIC LOCOMOTIVES

9005–9840   BRUSH/ABB   Bo-Bo-Bo

Built: 1993–2002 by Brush Traction, Loughborough.
Electric Supply System: 25 kV AC 50 Hz overhead.
Traction Motors: Asea Brown Boveri design. Asynchronous 3-phase motors. Model 6FHA 7059 (as built). Model 6FHA 7059C (7000 kW rated locos).
Maximum Tractive Effort: 400kN (90 000 lbf).
Continuous Rating: Class 9/0: 5760 kW (7725 hp). Class 9/7 and 9/8: 7000 kW (9387 hp).
Maximum Rail Power: **Multiple Working:** TDM system.
Brake Force: 50 t.   **Dimensions:** 22.01 x 2.97 x 4.20 m.
Weight: 136 t.   **Wheel Diameter:** 1250 mm.
Maximum Speed: 140 km/h.   **Design Speed:** 140 km/h.
Train Supply: Electric.   **Train Brakes:** Air.

Class 9/0 Original build locos. Built 1993–94.

9005	**EB**	ET	CO	JESSYE NORMAN

9007	**EB**	ET	CO	DAME JOAN SUTHERLAND[1]
9011	**EB**	ET	CO	JOSÉ VAN DAM[1]
9013	**EB**	ET	CO	MARIA CALLAS[1]
9015	**EB**	ET	CO	LÖTSCHBERG 1913[1]
9018	**EB**	ET	CO	WILHELMENIA FERNANDEZ
9022	**EB**	ET	CO	DAME JANET BAKER
9024	**EB**	ET	CO	GOTTHARD 1882
9026	**EB**	ET	CO	FURKATUNNEL 1982
9029	**EB**	ET	CO	THOMAS ALLEN
9033	**EB**	ET	CO	MONTSERRAT CABALLE
9036	**EB**	ET	CO	ALAIN FONDARY[1]
9037	**EB**	ET	CO	

Class 9/7. Increased power freight shuttle locos. Built 2001–02 (9711–23 built 1998–2001 as 9101–13 and rebuilt as 9711–23 2010–12).

9701		**EB**	ET	CO
9702		**EB**	ET	CO
9703		**EB**	ET	CO
9704		**EB**	ET	CO
9705		**EB**	ET	CO
9706		**EB**	ET	CO
9707		**EB**	ET	CO

9711	(9101)	**EB**	ET	CO
9712	(9102)	**EB**	ET	CO
9713	(9103)	**EB**	ET	CO
9714	(9104)	**EB**	ET	CO
9715	(9105)	**EB**	ET	CO
9716	(9106)	**EB**	ET	CO
9717	(9107)	**EB**	ET	CO
9718	(9108)	**EB**	ET	CO
9719	(9109)	**EB**	ET	CO
9720	(9110)	**EB**	ET	CO
9721	(9111)	**EB**	ET	CO
9722	(9112)	**EB**	ET	CO
9723	(9113)	**EB**	ET	CO

Class 9/8 Locos rebuilt from Class 9/0 by adding 800 to the loco number. Uprated to 7000 kW.

90xx and 98xx locomotives have a cab in the blunt end for shunting, except 9840 which does not have this feature.

9801	**EB**	ET	CO	LESLEY GARRETT
9802	**EB**	ET	CO	STUART BURROWS
9803	**EB**	ET	CO	BENJAMIN LUXON
9804	**EB**	ET	CO	
9806	**EB**	ET	CO	REGINE CRESPIN
9808	**EB**	ET	CO	ELISABETH SODERSTROM
9809	**EB**	ET	CO	
9810	**EB**	ET	CO	
9812	**EB**	ET	CO	
9814	**EB**	ET	CO	LUCIA POPP

9816	**EB**	ET	CO
9819	**EB**	ET	CO	MARIA EWING[1]
9820	**EB**	ET	CO	NICOLAI GHIAROV
9821	**EB**	ET	CO
9823	**EB**	ET	CO	DAME ELISABETH LEGGE-SCHWARZKOPF
9825	**EB**	ET	CO
9827	**EB**	ET	CO	BARBARA HENDRICKS
9828	**EB**	ET	CO
9831	**EB**	ET	CO
9832	**EB**	ET	CO	RENATA TEBALDI
9834	**EB**	ET	CO	MIRELLA FRENI
9835	**EB**	ET	CO	NICOLAI GEDDA
9838	**EB**	ET	CO	HILDEGARD BEHRENS
9840	**EB**	ET	CO

[1] nameplates carried on one side only.

4. LOCOMOTIVES AWAITING DISPOSAL

Locomotives that are still extant but best classed as awaiting disposal are listed here.

66048   EMD, Longport Works

5. LOCOMOTIVES EXPORTED FOR USE ABROAD

This section details former British Railways (plus privatisation era) diesel and electric locomotives that have been exported from Great Britain for use in industrial locations or with a main line operator abroad. Not included are locos that are classed as "preserved" abroad. These are included in the Platform 5 "Preserved Locomotives of British Railways" publication.

(S) denotes locomotives that are stored.

Number Other no./name   Location

Class 03

03156		Ferramenta Pugliese, Terlizzi, Bari, Italy

Class 47

47375	92 70 00 47375-5	Continental Railway Solution, Hungary

Class 56

56101	92 55 0659 001-5	FLOYD, Hungary
56115	92 55 0659 002-3	FLOYD, Hungary
56117	92 55 0659 003-1	FLOYD, Hungary (S) Budapest Keleti

Class 58

58001		DB, France, (S) Alizay
58004		DB, France, (S) Alizay
58005		DB, France, (S) Alizay
58006		DB, France, (S) Alizay
58007		DB, France, (S) Alizay
58009		DB, France, (S) Alizay
58010		DB, France, (S) Alizay
58011		DB, France, (S) Alizay
58013		DB, France, (S) Alizay
58018		DB, France, (S) Alizay
58021		DB, France, (S) Alizay
58025		DB, Spain, (S) Albacete
58026		DB, France, (S) Alizay
58027	L52	DB, Spain, (S) Albacete
58032		DB, France, (S) Alizay
58033		DB, France, (S) Alizay
58034		DB, France, (S) Alizay
58035		DB, France, (S) Alizay
58036		DB, France, (S) Alizay
58038		DB, France, (S) Alizay
58039		DB, France, (S) Alizay
58040		DB, France, (S) Alizay
58041	L36	Transfesa, Spain, (S) Albacete
58042		DB, France, (S) Alizay
58044		DB, France, (S) Woippy, Metz

58046		DB, France, (S) Alizay
58049		DB, France, (S) Alizay
58050	L53	DB, Spain, (S) Albacete

Class 66

66010	ECR, France	66195	ECR, France	66235		ECR, France
66022	ECR, France	66196	DBC, Poland	66236		ECR, France
66026	ECR, France	66201	ECR, France	66237		DBC, Poland
66028	ECR, France	66202	ECR, France	66239		ECR, France
66029	ECR, France	66203	ECR, France	66240		ECR, France
66032	ECR, France	66204	ECR, France	66241		ECR, France
66033	ECR, France	66205	ECR, France	66242		ECR, France
66036	ECR, France	66208	ECR, France	66243		ECR, France
66038	ECR, France	66209	ECR, France	66244		ECR, France
66042	ECR, France	66210	ECR, France	66245		ECR, France
66045	ECR, France	66211	ECR, France	66246		ECR, France
66049	ECR, France	66212	ECR, France	66247		ECR, France
66052	ECR, France	66213	ECR, France	66248		DBC, Poland
66062	ECR, France	66214	ECR, France	66249		ECR, France
66064	ECR, France	66215	ECR, France	66411	66013	FL, Poland
66071	ECR, France	66216	ECR, France	66412	66015	FL, Poland
66072	ECR, France	66217	ECR, France	66417	66016	FL, Poland
66073	ECR, France	66218	ECR, France	66527	66016	FL, Poland
66123	ECR, France	66219	ECR, France	66530	66017	FL, Poland
66146	DBC, Poland	66220	DBC, Poland	66535	66018	FL, Poland
66153	DBC, Poland	66222	ECR, France	66582	66009	FL, Poland
66157	DBC, Poland	66223	ECR, France	66583	66010	FL, Poland
66159	DBC, Poland	66224	ECR, France	66584	66011	FL, Poland
66163	DBC, Poland	66225	ECR, France	66586	66008	FL, Poland
66166	DBC, Poland	66226	ECR, France	66595		FL, Poland
66173	DBC, Poland	66227	DBC, Poland	66608	66603	FL, Poland
66178	DBC, Poland	66228	ECR, France	66609	66605	FL, Poland
66179	ECR, France	66229	ECR, France	66611	66604	FL, Poland
66180	DBC, Poland	66231	ECR, France	66612	66606	FL, Poland
66189	DBC, Poland	66232	ECR, France	66624	66602	FL, Poland
66190	ECR, France	66233	ECR, France	66625	66601	FL, Poland
66191	ECR, France	66234	ECR, France	66954		FL, Poland
66193	ECR, France					

Class 86

86213	91 52 00 87703-2 Lancashire Witch	Bulmarket, Bulgaria
86215	91 55 0450 005-8	FLOYD, Hungary
86217	91 55 0450 006-6	FLOYD, Hungary
86218	91 55 0450 004-1	FLOYD, Hungary
86228	91 55 0450 007-4	FLOYD, Hungary
86231	91 52 00 85005-4 Lady of the Lake	Bulmarket, Bulgaria
86232	91 55 0450 003-3	FLOYD, Hungary
86233		Bulmarket, Bulgaria (S) Ruse
86234		Bulmarket, Bulgaria
86235	91 52 00 87704-0 Novelty	Bulmarket, Bulgaria
86242	91 55 0450 008-2	FLOYD, Hungary

86248	91 55 0450 001-7		FLOYD, Hungary
86250	91 55 0450 002-5		FLOYD, Hungary
86424	91 55 0450 009-0		FLOYD, Hungary (S) Budapest
86701	91 52 00 87701-6	Orion	Bulmarket, Bulgaria
86702	91 52 00 87702-4	Cassiopeia	Bulmarket, Bulgaria

Class 87

87003	91 52 00 87003-7		BZK, Bulgaria
87004	91 52 00 87004-5	Britannia	BZK, Bulgaria
87006	91 52 00 87006-0		BZK, Bulgaria
87007	91 52 00 87007-8		BZK, Bulgaria
87008	87008-9		BZK, Bulgaria (S) Ruse
87009	91 52 00 87009-4		Bulmarket, Bulgaria
87010	91 52 00 87010-2		BZK, Bulgaria
87012	91 52 00 87012-8		BZK, Bulgaria
87013	91 52 00 87013-6		BZK, Bulgaria
87014	87014-7		BZK, Bulgaria (S) Sofia
87017	91 52 00 87017-7	Iron Duke	Bulmarket, Bulgaria
87019	91 52 00 87019-3		BZK, Bulgaria
87020	91 52 00 87020-1		BZK, Bulgaria
87022	91 52 00 87022-7		BZK, Bulgaria
87023	91 52 00 87023-5	Velocity	Bulmarket, Bulgaria
87025	91 52 00 87025-0		Bulmarket, Bulgaria
87026	91 52 00 87026-8		BZK, Bulgaria
87028	91 52 00 87028-4		BZK, Bulgaria
87029	91 52 00 87029-2		BZK, Bulgaria
87033	91 52 00 87033-4		BZK, Bulgaria
87034	91 52 00 87034-2		BZK, Bulgaria

Class 92

92001	91 53 0 472 002-1	Mircea Eliade	Transagent Rail, Croatia
92002	91 53 0 472 003-9	Lucian Blaga	Transagent Rail, Croatia
92003		Beethoven	DB Cargo, Romania (S)
92005	91 53 0 472-005-4		Transagent Rail, Croatia
92012	91 53 0 472 001-3	Mihai Eminescu	Transagent Rail, Croatia
92022		Charles Dickens	DB Cargo, Bulgaria (S) Aurubis
92024	91 53 0 472 004-7	Marin Preda	Transagent Rail, Croatia
92025	91 52 1 688 025-1	Oscar Wilde	DB Cargo, Bulgaria
92026		Britten	DB Cargo, Romania
92027	91 52 1 688 027-7	George Eliot	DB Cargo, Bulgaria
92030	91 52 1 688 030-1	Ashford	DB Cargo, Bulgaria
92034	91 52 1 688 034-3	Kipling	DB Cargo, Bulgaria
92039	91 53 0 472 006-2	Eugen Ionescu	DB Cargo, Romania

6. CODES

6.1. LIVERY CODES

Livery codes are used to denote the various liveries carried. It is impossible to list every livery variation which currently exists. In particular, items ignored for this publication include minor colour variations, omission of logos and all numbering, lettering and brandings. Descriptions quoted are thus a general guide only. Logos as appropriate for each livery are normally deemed to be carried. The colour of the lower half of the bodyside is stated first.

AB   Arriva Trains Wales/Welsh Government sponsored dark blue.
AI   Aggregate Industries (green, light grey & blue).
AL   Advertising/promotional livery (see class heading for details).
AR   Anglia Railways (turquoise blue with a white stripe).
AW   Arriva Trains Wales/Welsh Government sponsored dark & light blue.
AZ   Advenza Freight (deep blue with green Advenza brandings).
B   BR blue.
BL   BR Revised blue with yellow cabs, grey roof, large numbers & logo.
CA   Caledonian Sleeper (dark blue).
CD   Cotswold Rail (silver with blue & red logo).
CE   BR Civil Engineers (yellow & grey with black cab doors & window surrounds).
CM   Chiltern Mainline loco-hauled (two-tone grey & silver with blue stripes).
CS   Colas Rail (yellow, orange & black).
CU   Corus (silver with red logos).
DB   DB Cargo (Deutsche Bahn red with grey roof and solebar).
DC   Devon & Cornwall Railways (metallic silver).
DG   BR Departmental (dark grey with black cab doors & window surrounds).
DI   New DRS {Class 68 style} (deep blue & aquamarine with compass logo).
DR   Direct Rail Services (dark blue with light blue or dark grey roof).
DS   Revised Direct Rail Services (dark blue, light blue & green. "Compass" logo).
E   English Welsh & Scottish Railway (maroon bodyside & roof with a broad gold bodyside band).
EA   East Midlands Trains revised HST (dark blue, orange & red).
EB   Eurotunnel (two-tone grey with a broad blue stripe).
EG   "EWS grey" (as **F** but with large yellow & red EWS logo).
EP   European Passenger Services (two-tone grey with dark blue roof).
EX   Europhoenix (silver, blue & red).
F   BR Trainload Freight (two-tone grey with black cab doors & window surrounds. Various logos).
FA   Fastline Freight (grey & black with white & orange stripes).
FB   First Group dark blue.
FE   Railfreight Distribution International (two tone-grey with black cab doors & dark blue roof).
FER   Fertis (light grey with a dark grey roof & solebar).
FF   Freightliner grey (two-tone grey with black cab doors & window surrounds. Freightliner logo).
FG   New Freightliner; Genesee & Wyoming style (orange with black & yellow lower bodyside stripes).

FH   Revised Freightliner {PowerHaul} (dark green with yellow ends & a grey stripe/buffer beam).
FL   Freightliner (dark green with yellow cabs).
FO   BR Railfreight (grey bodysides, yellow cabs & red lower bodyside stripe, large BR logo).
FR   Fragonset Railways (black with silver roof & a red bodyside band lined out in white).
FS   First Group (indigo blue with pink & white stripes).
G   BR Green (plain green, with white stripe on main line locomotives).
GA   Greater Anglia (white with a black stripe).
GB   GB Railfreight (blue with orange cantrail & solebar stripes, orange cabs).
GC   Grand Central (all over black with an orange stripe).
GG   BR green (two-tone green).
GL   First Great Western locomotives (green with a gold stripe).
GW   Great Western Railway (TOC) dark green.
GY   Eurotunnel (grey & yellow).
HA   Hanson Quarry Products (dark blue/silver with oxide red roof).
HN   Harry Needle Railroad Company (orange with a black roof and solebar).
HU   Hunslet Engine Company (dark blue & orange).
IC   BR InterCity (dark grey/white/red/white).
K   Black.
KB   Knorr-Bremse Rail UK (blue, white & light green).
LH   BR Loadhaul (black with orange cabsides).
LM   London Midland (white/grey & green with broad black stripe around the windows).
LW   LNWR (grey with a red solebar).
M   Maroon.
ML   BR Mainline Freight (aircraft blue with a silver stripe).
MT   Maritime (blue with white lettering).
N   BR Network SouthEast (white & blue with red lower bodyside stripe, grey solebar & cab ends).
O   Non-standard (see class heading for details).
PC   Pullman Car Company (umber & cream with gold lettering lined out in gold).
RB   Riviera Trains Oxford blue.
RL   RMS Locotec (dark blue with light grey cabsides).
RO   Rail Operations Group (dark blue).
RS   Railway Support Services (grey with a red solebar).
RX   Rail Express Systems (dark grey & red with or without blue markings).
RZ   Royal Train revised (plain claret, no lining).
SL   Silverlink (indigo blue with white stripe, green lower body & yellow doors).
SI   ScotRail InterCity (light grey & dark blue with INTER7CITY branding).
SN   Southern (white & dark green with light green semi-circles at one end of each vehicle. Light grey band at solebar level).
SR   ScotRail – Scotland's Railways (dark blue with Scottish Saltire flag & white/light blue flashes).
ST   Stagecoach (blue with red cabs).
TP   TransPennine Express (silver, grey, blue & purple).
TT   Transmart Trains (all over green).
TW   Transport for Wales (white with a red cantrail stripe and grey lower bodyside stripe).

V	Virgin Trains (red with black doors extending into bodysides, three white lower bodyside stripes).
VE	Virgin Trains East Coast (red & white with black window surrounds).
VN	Belmond Northern Belle (crimson lake & cream lined out in gold).
VP	Virgin Trains shunters (black with a large black & white chequered flag on the bodyside).
WA	Wabtec Rail (black).
WC	West Coast Railway Company maroon.
XC	CrossCountry (two-tone silver with deep crimson ends and pink doors).
Y	Network Rail yellow.

6.2. OWNER CODES

The following codes are used to define the ownership details of the locomotives or rolling stock listed in this book. Codes shown indicate either the legal owner or "responsible custodian" of each vehicle.

125	125 Group
20	Class 20189
37	Scottish Thirty-Seven Group
40	Class 40 Preservation Society
47	Stratford 47 Group
50	Class 50 Alliance
56	Class 56 Locomotives
70	7029 Clun Castle
71	71A Locomotives
2L	Class Twenty Locomotives
A	Angel Trains
AD	AV Dawson
AF	Arlington Fleet Services
AK	Akiem
AM	Alstom
AV	Arriva UK Trains
BD	Bardon Aggregates
BN	Beacon Rail
BT	Bombardier Transportation
CD	Crewe Diesel Preservation Group
CS	Colas Rail
D0	D05 Preservation Group
DA	Data Acquisition & Testing Services
DB	DB Cargo (UK)
DC	DC Rail
DP	Deltic Preservation Society
DR	Direct Rail Services
DT	The Diesel Traction Group
E	Eversholt Rail (UK)
EE	English Electric Preservation
EL	Electric Traction Limited
EM	East Midlands Railway

EO   ElectroMotive Diesel Services
EP   Europhoenix
ET   Eurotunnel
EU   Eurostar International
EY   European Metal Recycling
FG   First Group
FL   Freightliner
GB   GB Railfreight
GW   Great Western Railway (assets of the Greater Western franchise)
HH   Hanson & Hall Rail Services
HN   Harry Needle Railroad Company
HU   Hunslet Engine Company
LF   Lombard Finance
LN   London Overground
LO   Loram (UK)
LS   Locomotive Services
ME   Meteor Power
MR   Mendip Rail
NB   Boden Rail Engineering
NM   National Museum of Science & Industry
NR   Network Rail
NS   Nemesis Rail
NY   North Yorkshire Moors Railway Enterprises
P   Porterbrook Leasing Company
PO   Other private owner
PP   Peter Pan Locomotive Company
RL   Rail Management Services (trading as RMS Locotec)
RO   Rail Operations Group
RS   Railway Support Services
RV   Riviera Trains
RU   Russell Logistics
SB   Steve Beniston
SP   The Scottish Railway Preservation Society
ST   Shaun Wright
SU   SembCorp Utilities UK
TT   Transmart Trains
UR   UK Rail Leasing
VG   Victoria Group
WA   Wabtec Rail Group
WC   West Coast Railway Company
WM   West Midlands Trains

6.3. LOCOMOTIVE POOL CODES

Locomotives are split into operational groups ("pools") for diagramming and maintenance purposes. The codes used to denote these pools are shown in this publication.

AWCA   West Coast Railway Company operational locomotives.
AWCX   West Coast Railway Company stored locomotives.

CFOL	Class 50 Operations locomotives.
CFSL	Class 40 Preservation Society Locomotives.
COFS	Colas Rail Class 56.
COLO	Colas Rail Classes 66 & 70.
COLS	Colas Rail stored locomotives.
COTS	Colas Rail Classes 37 & 67.
DCRO	DC Rail Class 50 & 56.
DCRS	DC Rail Class 60.
DFGI	Freightliner Class 70.
DFHG	Freightliner Class 59.
DFHH	Freightliner Class 66/6.
DFIM	Freightliner Class 66/5.
DFIN	Freightliner low emission Class 66.
DFLC	Freightliner Class 90.
DFNC	Freightliner Class 86/6.
DHLT	Freightliner locomotives awaiting maintenance/repair/disposal.
EFOO	Great Western Railway Class 57.
EFPC	Great Western Railway 43.
EHPC	CrossCountry Class 43.
EMPC	East Midlands Railway Class 43.
EPEX	Europhoenix locomotives for export.
EPUK	Europhoenix UK locomotives.
GBBR	GB Railfreight Class 73 for possible rebuilding.
GBBT	GB Railfreight Class 66. Large fuel tanks.
GBCH	GB Railfreight Class 86.
GBCS	GB Railfreight Class 73/9. Caledonian Sleeper.
GBCT	GB Railfreight Class 92. Channel Tunnel traffic.
GBDF	GB Railfreight Class 47.
GBEB	GB Railfreight Class 66. Ex-European, large fuel tanks.
GBED	GB Railfreight Class 73.
GBEE	GB Railfreight Class 20.
GBEL	GB Railfreight Class 66. New build, small fuel tanks.
GBFM	GB Railfreight Class 66. RETB fitted.
GBGD	GB Railfreight Class 56. Operational locomotives.
GBGS	GB Railfreight Class 56. Stored locomotives.
GBLT	GB Railfreight Class 66. Small fuel tanks.
GBNB	GB Railfreight Class 66. New build.
GBNR	GB Railfreight Class 73/9. Network Rail contracts.
GBOB	GB Railfreight Class 66. Former DB Cargo locomotives; large fuel tanks and buckeye couplers.
GBSD	GB Railfreight. Stored locomotives.
GBSL	GB Railfreight Class 92. Caledonian Sleeper.
GBST	GB Railfreight Class 92. Caledonian Sleeper & Channel Tunnel.
GBTG	GB Railfreight Class 60.
GBYH	GB Railfreight Class 59.
GROG	Rail Operations Group operational locomotives.
HAPC	ScotRail Class 43.
HNRL	Harry Needle Railroad Company hire locomotives.
HNRS	Harry Needle Railroad Company stored locomotives.
HTLX	Hanson & Hall Rail Services locomotives.
HYWD	South Western Railway Class 73.

IANA	Greater Anglia Class 90.
IECA	London North Eastern Railway Class 91.
IECP	London North Eastern Railway Class 43.
LSLO	Locomotive Services operational locomotives.
LSLS	Locomotive Services stored locomotives.
MBDL	Non TOC-owned diesel locomotives.
MBED	Non TOC-owned electro-diesel locomotives.
MBEL	Non TOC-owned electric locomotives.
MOLO	Class 20189 Ltd Class 20.
NRLO	Nemesis Rail locomotives.
QADD	Network Rail locomotives.
QCAR	Network Rail New Measurement Train Class 43.
QETS	Network Rail Class 37.
RAJV	Scottish Railway Preservation Society Class 37.
SAXL	Eversholt Rail off-lease locomotives.
SBXL	Porterbrook Leasing Company stored locomotives.
SCEL	Angel Trains stored locomotives.
SROG	Rail Operations Group locomotives under overhaul.
TPEX	TransPennine Express Class 68 locomotives.
UKRL	UK Rail Leasing. Operational locomotives.
UKRM	UK Rail Leasing. Locomotives for overhaul.
UKRS	UK Rail Leasing. Stored locomotives.
WAAC	DB Cargo Class 67.
WABC	DB Cargo Class 67. RETB fitted.
WACC	DB Cargo Class 67 for hire to Transport for Wales.
WBAE	DB Cargo Class 66. Locomotives fitted with "stop-start" technology.
WBAR	DB Cargo Class 66. Fitted with remote monitoring equipment.
WBAT	DB Cargo Class 66.
WBBE	DB Cargo Class 66. RETB fitted and fitted with "stop-start" technology.
WBBT	DB Cargo Class 66. RETB fitted.
WBLE	DB Cargo Class 66. Dedicated locomotives for Lickey Incline banking duties. Fitted with "stop-start" technology.
WCAT	DB Cargo Class 60.
WCBT	DB Cargo Class 60. Extended-range fuel tanks.
WEAC	DB Cargo Class 90.
WEDC	DB Cargo Class 90. Modified for operation with Mark 4s.
WFBC	DB Cargo Class 92 with TVM430 cab signalling equipment for use on High Speed 1.
WQAA	DB Cargo stored locomotives Group 1A (short-term maintenance).
WQAB	DB Cargo stored locomotives Group 1B.
WQBA	DB Cargo stored locomotives Group 2 (unserviceable).
WQCA	DB Cargo stored locomotives Group 3 (unserviceable).
WQDA	DB Cargo stored locomotives Group 4 (awaiting disposal).
XHAC	Direct Rail Services Classes 37/4 & 57/3.
XHCE	Direct Rail Services Class 68 for hire to Chiltern Railways.
XHCK	Direct Rail Services Classes 20 & 57/0.
XHIM	Direct Rail Services locomotives – Intermodal traffic.
XHNC	Direct Rail Services locomotives – nuclear traffic/general.
XHSS	Direct Rail Services stored locomotives.
XHVE	Direct Rail Services Classes 68 & 88.
XHVT	Direct Rail Services Class 57/3 for hire to Avanti West Coast.

6.4. ALLOCATION & LOCATION CODES

Allocation codes are used in this publication to denote the normal maintenance base ("depots") of each operational locomotive. However, maintenance may be carried out at other locations and also by mobile teams. The designation (S) denotes stored.

Code	Location	Depot Operator
BH	Barrow Hill (Chesterfield)	Barrow Hill Engine Shed Society
BL	Shackerstone, Battlefield Line	*Storage location only*
BM	Bournemouth	South Western Railway
BN	Bounds Green (London)	Hitachi
BO	Bo'ness (West Lothian)	The Bo'ness & Kinneil Railway
BQ	Bury (Greater Manchester)	East Lancashire Railway Trust
BU	Burton-upon-Trent	Nemesis Rail
CB	Crewe Basford Hall	Freightliner Engineering
CE	Crewe International	DB Cargo (UK)
CF	Cardiff Canton	Transport for Wales/Colas Rail
CL	Crewe LNWR Heritage	LNWR Heritage Company
CO	Coquelles (France)	Eurotunnel
CR	Crewe Gresty Bridge	Direct Rail Services
CS	Carnforth	West Coast Railway Company
CT	Cheriton (Folkestone)	Eurotunnel
DR	Doncaster Belmont Yard/RMT	*Storage location only*
DY	Derby Etches Park	East Midlands Railway
EC	Edinburgh Craigentinny	Hitachi
EP	Ely Papworth Sidings	*Storage location only*
GA	Gascoigne Wood Sidings (South Milford)	*Storage location only*
HA	Haymarket (Edinburgh)	ScotRail
HO	Hope Cement Works	Breedon Hope Cement
HJ	Hoo Junction (Kent)	Colas Rail
KM	Carlisle Kingmoor	Direct Rail Services
KR	Kidderminster	Severn Valley Railway
LA	Laira (Plymouth)	Great Western Railway
LB	Loughborough Works	Brush Traction
LD	Leeds Midland Road	Freightliner Engineering
LM	Quinton Rail Technology Centre (Long Marston, Warwickshire)	Motorail Logistics
LR	Leicester	UK Rail Leasing
LT	Longport (Stoke-on-Trent)	ElectroMotive Diesel Services
LW	MoD Longtown (Cumbria)	*Storage location only*
MD	Merehead	Mendip Rail
NC	Norwich Crown Point	Greater Anglia
NL	Neville Hill (Leeds)	East Midlands Railway/Northern
NM	Nottingham Eastcroft	East Midlands Railway/Boden Rail
NY	Grosmont (North Yorkshire)	North Yorkshire Moors Railway Enterprises
PZ	Penzance Long Rock	Great Western Railway
RJ	Rectory Junction (Nottingham)	Data Acquisition & Testing Services
RR	Doncaster Robert's Road	ElectroMotive Diesel Services
RU	Rugby	Colas Rail
SC	Scunthorpe Steelworks	British Steel

SE	St Leonards (Hastings)	St Leonards Railway Engineering
SL	Stewarts Lane (London)	Govia Thameslink Railway/Belmond
SK	Swanwick West (Derbyshire)	The Princess Royal Locomotive Trust
SW	Swanage	Swanage Railway
TM	Tyseley Locomotive Works	Vintage Trains
TO	Toton (Nottinghamshire)	DB Cargo (UK)
WB	Wembley (London)	Alstom
WN	Willesden (London)	Bombardier Transportation
WS	Worksop (Nottinghamshire)	Harry Needle Railroad Company
YK	National Railway Museum (York)	National Museum of Science & Industry

ZA	RTC Business Park (Derby)	LORAM (UK)
ZB	Doncaster Works	Wabtec Rail
ZC	Crewe Works	Bombardier Transportation UK
ZD	Derby Works	Bombardier Transportation UK
ZG	Eastleigh Works	Arlington Fleet Services
ZH	Springburn Depot (Glasgow)	*Closed, storage location only*
ZI	Ilford Works	Bombardier Transportation UK
ZJ	Stoke-on-Trent Works	Axiom Rail (Stoke)
ZK	Kilmarnock Caledonia Works	Brodie Engineering
ZM	Kilmarnock Bonnyton Works	Brodie Engineering
ZN	Wolverton Works	Gemini Rail Group
ZR	Holgate Works (York)	Network Rail